UNSTOPPABLE.

The Mentally Tough Gymnast

Julie Jankowski, M.S.

ISBN: 1977635148
ISBN-13: 978-1977635143

DEDICATION

To my family who has always celebrated my performances, win or lose.

To my husband for his unconditional support of my dreams.

To my sons Easton and Brody for showing me what is truly important in life.

To my gymnastics family who make my job not feel like a job at all.

CONTENTS

PREFACE

This book was written for the gymnast who is the first to arrive and last to leave.

This is for the gymnast on the sidelines, just dying to get out and perform.

This is for the gymnast who does extra pushups than is required.

This is for the gymnast who struggles through each day, just trying to get back what they had.

This is for the gymnast who is determined to not let setbacks get in their way.

This is for the gymnast who is tired of letting their fear take control.

This is for the gymnast trying to find the fighter inside themselves.

This is for the gymnast who not only wants to succeed, but make history in the process.

This is for the gymnast who is not afraid to make mistakes.

This is for the gymnast who is not satisfied with being ordinary.

This is for you.

Not too terribly long ago, I was you. I felt like I had to work twice as hard as everyone just to make it through practice. Any steps I took forward were followed by five steps back. I fell down too many times to count. Bruised, literally and emotionally, I got up every time to face another day, even though I wanted to crawl in a corner and cry.

It was as if there was a brick wall blocking my way. There was no way around it, it went for miles. No way over it, another layer of bricks was added anytime I climbed my way up. No way through it, the bricks cut my hands as I punched them. Words were scrawled on it, "You can't do it." Waiting and hoping the wall would fall down didn't work. If I asked politely for a way to the other side, it laughed at me. Yelling and screaming made it even tougher. *There has to be a better way*, I thought.

Then a stroke of brilliance. I had been so busy focusing on trying to change the wall, I had disregarded that I may need to change myself. I had no confidence to speak of, no motivation, no goals, and only focused on the negatives. How could I expect to break down a brick wall being that way? I asked myself why I was still here, what did I want out of this?" I looked at myself in the mirror and didn't like who I saw. Gradually I made changes in myself to become more like the person I wanted to be, and gradually the bricks fell down one by one. The wall didn't fall down all at once, it still took a lot of time and effort on my part. I had inadvertently put the wall up myself and it was up to me to take it down.
Now I stand tall before you, with nothing blocking my way. There's no stopping me now. I am **unstoppable.**

This book will help you on your quest to become an unstoppable, mentally tough gymnast. Many self-help sport psychology books tell you all about a topic or skill, why it's important you should have it, theories about why it works, quizzes to see if you need to work on it, and then gives you five sentences of advice on how to deal with your problem. That may be because if they give you all their secrets, you won't need them to counsel you. Maybe they'll give you a taste of it, but don't let you have the whole pie so you keep coming back for more. That's not me. If after reading my book you don't need me to consult with you, then I've done my job. You don't need the top 200 mental toughness skills. What I have written for you is a no nonsense, interactive, fix-me-now sort of book.

In this book, you will learn the sport psychology skills I feel are most important for success. I suggest reading through from start to finish, however the chapters can stand alone. A unique aspect of this book is that you can skip to the chapter you need at the moment. If you need to learn about focus first, you can do that. However, I strongly suggest you go back and read through the other chapters in order to become a mentally tough gymnast. Just because you learned how to focus doesn't make you unstoppable. Also, make sure you actually do the activities and exercises; I didn't put them in there for show. I can tell you about goals, and I can show you charts for goals, but not until you actually fill out the chart will you fully understand. It is a strong statement to say you are mentally tough or unstoppable, and breezing through the chapters will not automatically make you a success.

I foresee many benefits for you as a gymnast. Not only do I see an improvement in your gymnastics performance, but also a happier you. I see someone who is confident and knows what they want, and is motivated and willing to go the distance. I see someone who enjoys gymnastics and loves the thrill of competition, someone who has taken control of their life and won't take no for an answer. **I see someone who is a success.**

PART 1:
Understanding Mental Toughness

CHAPTER 1
MENTAL TOUGHNESS DEFINED

Imagine someone with complete confidence without arrogance, the courage of a lion, the persistence of a child asking why, the motivation of a hungry animal, the composure of a king or queen, and precision focus of a hawk. This is a vision of a mentally tough athlete. "Mental toughness" is a term that you cannot find in the dictionary, and therefore its true meaning is disputed and usually described by a laundry list of adjectives and qualities one must possess. The literature on sport psychology uses a variation of similar words to define mental toughness. The characteristics that repeat themselves among the research (Creasy, 2006; Fourie, 2001; Jones, 2002; Scarnati, 2000; Siebold, 2005; Yukelson, 2008) are:

courage, confidence, motivation, composure, focus, and perseverance

I sum up these six characteristics with one powerful word:

UNSTOPPABLE.

No one can stop you from succeeding.

Nothing can get in the way of your dreams.

No mistake can shake you.

No challenge will prevent you from achieving greatness.

*You are **unstoppable**.*

ACTIVITY

What characteristics or skills would you include when you think of yourself as unstoppable?

Determined	confident
Fearless	courageous
persistent	empowered
Focused	fighter
resilient	driven

Vision of an Unstoppable Gymnast

The advantages of becoming a mentally tough, unstoppable gymnast are endless and the value of each characteristic or skill is priceless. Just imagine how it might feel being unstoppable. Your confidence has never been higher and you feel like you could easily take on any task. Your mind and body are poised for performing; you are eager to get out there and just do what you love doing. You feel optimistic that you and your team will be successful; the thought of failure never even crossed your mind.

When performing, you know you have an advantage over your opponents and you thrive on that. Competition is thrilling for you and only increases the quality of your performance. You have complete confidence, an emotional strength to continue believing in yourself whether others do or doubt you. You have special talents that make you better than the rest. You have the mental hardiness to be brave in the face of fear and the courage to fight when others would back down from an intimidating challenge. You have a strong desire and passion for gymnastics. Setbacks only increase your determination to keep going.

You hold yourself at a higher level to achieve success and stay poised and calm in adverse conditions. You can manage your anxiety and handle pressure effectively while others let it take over control. You do not dwell on mistakes, you simply look for the next productive action. You have the ability to intensely block out distractions and negativity. Unexpected events do not faze you; you always have your next move planned. You push through physically and psychologically demanding training while maintaining consistent technique and effort. You expect more from yourself and therefore receive more in return. You are great and you know it.

Since everyone needs their own personal definition of mental toughness, I arrive at this definition:

> *Men-tal Tough-ness (n.):*
> *a. One who possesses emotional strength, strong desire, psychological hardiness, and poise under pressure, which allows the individual to have a psychological advantage over their opponents.*
> *b. One who is unstoppable.*

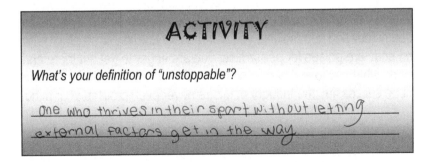

ACTIVITY

What's your definition of "unstoppable"?

one who thrives in their sport without letting external factors get in the way.

CHAPTER 2
CHARACTERISTICS OF ELITE ATHLETES

There is something that sets apart the great athletes from the good, first place from second place, perfection from mistakes. There has been a lot of research to determine what that "something" is, what specific psychological characteristics and skills elite athletes possess that others do not have. To become an unstoppable gymnast you need to know what you're up against; what characteristics other mentally tough gymnasts are working with and can use to their advantage. The second part of the book will help you strive to obtain these qualities and skills.

Researchers have found that most of the athletes in their studies possess many admirable traits and psychological skills, with the *elite* athletes generally having higher levels of those traits. They determined that there are many traits that are useful for becoming an elite athlete and predicting potential success for an athlete. However, six characteristics were repeated several times as characteristics that set apart the elite athletes.

According to Elferink (2004), Gould (1992, 1999, 2002), Meyers (1996, 1999), Reilly (2000), Ungerleider (1991), and Williams (2000), the elite athletes had significantly higher levels of:

MOTIVATION *Confidence*

Anxiety Management skills

Concentration Anticipation

Visualization skills

Interesting how many of these are included in the definitions of mental toughness. Not a coincidence!

To determine the characteristics of elite athletes, the preferred method was administering psychological assessments or questionnaires (Elferink, 2004; Mahoney, 1977; Meyers, 1996; Meyers, 1999; Reilly, 2000; Williams, 2000). Many of the athletes in the studies were given the Psychological Skills Inventory for Sports (PSIS), Profile of Mood States (POMS), the Task and Ego Orientation in Sport Questionnaire (TEOSQ) by Duda (1989), and the modified trait-based version of the Competitive State Anxiety Inventory-2 (CSAI-2) by Jones and Swain (1995).

Additional characteristics and skills of elite athletes that were brought up in the literature by Gould (1992, 1999, 2002), Reilly (2000), Wang (2003), and Williams (2000) were:

maintaining composure BETTER DECISION-MAKING SKILLS

being task-oriented adjusting tactically (having a plan)

positive self-talk *believing in success* **commitment**

HAVING A SUPPORT SYSTEM **goal setting skills**

performance analysis

CHAPTER 3
MENTAL TRAINING PROGRAMS

A Mental Training Program (MTP) is a program to develop various sport psychology skills in order to improve an athlete's overall mental skills. It is much like your gymnastics practice. Mental skills need to be taught and practiced just like any physical skill. Part 2 of this book is meant to be a Mental Training Program. Read through each section, do the activities, follow the instructions, and you will be well on your way to becoming a mentally tough and unstoppable gymnast. Let's start with some ground rules:

Mental Training Rules

1. **Try Try Again**
   Learning sport psychology skills takes time and practice. The first rule states that you must try the skills and activities several times. You can't expect to master any physical gymnastics skill on the first try; mental skills are just the same.

2. **Practice Before Performance**
   The second rule states that you must practice the skills you learn today at home or at practice *before* using them in a competition setting. You are already under pressure during a competition and that is not the time to try out something new for the first time.

Practice the skills in a calm environment where you won't be penalized if you make a few mental mistakes. Use the skills in competition when you can use it without much thought.

3. **Buffet Rule**
   The third rule states that sport psychology skills are like a buffet. Many skills will be introduced to you in this book. Try all the skills and activities a couple times, but then just keep going back for what you like. Every person is different. Take with you what works, leave what doesn't.

MTP Skills

The ten most common sport psychology concepts and skills are: anxiety, communication, confidence, focus, goal setting, leadership, mental toughness, motivation, team building, and visualization. An MTP is an individual training program, and communication, leadership, and team building are based upon on other people. These skills will not immediately help you become a mentally tough gymnast and therefore were left out of the MTP.

These eight sport psychology concepts, the six characteristics from the mental toughness definition research, and the six psychological characteristics of elite athletes were all taken into consideration and combined into seven MTP skills. In your MTP, you will be learning to:

build your confidence and increase courage,

increase motivation and determination,

set effective goals,

visualize success,

reduce anxiety and improve composure,

increase focus and anticipation skills,

and develop perseverance.

Pre-Performance Routines

A pre-performance routine (PPR) is just that: a routine before your routine; It is your *mental* routine before your gymnastics routine. A pre-performance routine should be used in multiple occasions: before competitions, before each competitive event, before routines in practice, and before difficult skills.

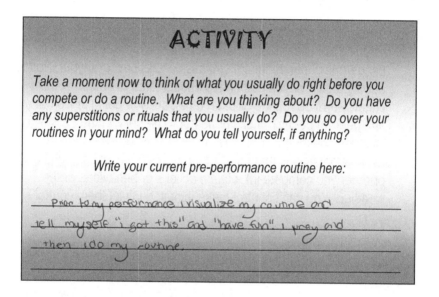

ACTIVITY

Take a moment now to think of what you usually do right before you compete or do a routine. What are you thinking about? Do you have any superstitions or rituals that you usually do? Do you go over your routines in your mind? What do you tell yourself, if anything?

Write your current pre-performance routine here:

Prior to my performance I visualize my routine and tell myself "i got this" and "have fun". I pray and then i do my routine.

Guidelines for Pre-Performance Routines

- **Keep it Short-** You usually won't have too much time to mentally prepare for a competition. A long drawn out routine is a burden to do right before competition and may drain you of energy. Make it less than 5 minutes long. Don't include the team warm-up and stretch in this time-frame, the PPR is just about you. **Please note:** The pre-competition PPR may have a few added actions such as listening to music, reading, or journaling that you would obviously not be doing right before your actual routine. *The pre-performance routine for immediately before a routine or a difficult skill is the same routine as your pre-competition PPR, just quicker and more condensed.*

- **Keep it Consistent and Comforting-** A consistent routine creates confidence and comfort. Doing something the same way each time will help your mind settle down into familiar territory and calm the nerves. Find what is comforting to you and do it each time before you compete. This could be listening to music, talking to teammates or family, observing the competition area, visualizing your performance, reciting a favorite inspirational quote, doing a team cheer, etc.

- **Avoid Uncontrollable Superstitions-** Lucky socks, rituals, or listening to the same song are okay, but can easily become a dangerous dependence. If you misplace your socks, your iPod is out of battery, or you don't have enough time to do that special cheer, warm up routine or other ritual, are you going to flip out and perform poorly? Let's hope not. The point of the PPR is to increase confidence, not crush it if it doesn't go your way. Also, avoid superstitions that focus on numbers (competition number or order you compete in), other's actions or behaviors, or the weather. You can't control these things, don't let them control you.

Mini MTP

The pre-performance routine should end up being a mini-MTP. All the mental skills you are learning in this book should ideally end up in your PPR as a last-minute mental training program before you compete, do a routine in practice, or perform a difficult skill. At the end of each chapter, there is a spot to choose a skill from the chapter to add into your pre-performance routine that will improve the quality of your performance.

PART 2:
Becoming Unstoppable

CHAPTER 4
CONFIDENCE

In This Chapter

- Benefits of Confidence
- Importance of Confidence
- Self-Fulfilling Prophecy
- Self-Concept
- Courage
- Confidence Building Strategies

Benefits of Being a Confident Gymnast

- Remain calm and relaxed under pressure
- Focus on the task at hand
- Put forth your best effort in any situation
- Set challenging goals
- Go after what you want
- Be highly motivated
- Succeed!

Importance of Confidence

One must start and end with confidence. If you have a low level of focusing skills, you can possibly make up for it with high motivation and high confidence. If you have a low level of visualization skills, you can still have high goal setting skills and high focusing skills. However, if you have low confidence, it affects all of your all other skills. You will have low motivation because you don't believe you will succeed whether you try or not, you will either not have any goals set in place or easier goals because you think you can't achieve any more than that, trouble with visualization and focus and because all you see is mistakes, and high anxiety because you are constantly worried about what others think of you.

> *"If you think you can, or you think you can't, you're right."*
> *-Henry Ford*

If I asked you to touch the moon, you probably would think you couldn't. You might reach up to the sky, feel silly, put your hand back down, and never try again. You didn't believe you could touch the moon, so you gave up. However, if you truly believed you could touch the moon, you would put everything you had into this dream, become an astronaut, and go to the moon. The point is, you must first believe you can become a great gymnast in order to become one. Learning to focus, visualize, or set goals just won't work if you don't start believing this will work.

Self-Fulfilling Prophecy

The thoughts you have about yourself cause a chain reaction and affect everything else down the line. It is called the Self-Fulfilling Prophecy.

It starts with a thought.
Thoughts affect your behavior.
Your behavior affects your performance.
Your performance confirms your original thoughts.

Let's take this scenario: A gymnast says "I haven't been hitting my bar routine in practice, so I'm probably not going to do well on bars today." Because she has already decided (subconsciously or consciously) she isn't going to do well, she half-heartedly warms up and doesn't fully get herself prepared for the meet. She isn't focusing on her skills or staying tight. Because she didn't prepare well, her performance suffers and she falls twice. The bad performance now reinforces her original thought. "See, I knew I wouldn't do well."

ACTIVITY

*Let's see how the Self-Fulfilling Prophecy can work **in your favor**:*

1. Think of a <u>positive thought</u> about your performance on an event you are struggling with: I work really hard I deserve to do well!

2. How will this affect your behavior/warm up? Motivate me

3. How will this affect your performance? Encourage me

4. How will this affect your original thought? It changes

Keep thinking positive thoughts to keep the cycle going to continue increasing your confidence!

Self-Concept

Your self-concept is the perception you have of yourself. This is a completely honest opinion of yourself, positive or negative. It is how you see yourself overall in the world, not how you feel specifically today. You can have good days and bad days, good moments and bad moments within those days, but self-concept is an average of how you normally feel overall.

ACTIVITY

*Using the Self-Concept explanation you just read, think of 8 words that describe you and write them down in the circles of the "Current Self-Concept." (Figure A) These could describe your personality, skills, or characteristics. Now write down 8 words that you **wish** would describe you- descriptions of your ideal self in the "Perfect Self" circle.*

Now compare the two sets of words. Are they similar? Are they opposites? The goal is to eventually make these two sets of words as similar as possible. The closer the current descriptions are to the perfect self descriptions, the higher one's self-confidence is. If there are substantial differences between the two descriptions, pin point those differences and work on ways to make them more similar.

Example: <u>Difference:</u> *Current Self-Concept is quiet and Perfect Self is out-going.* <u>How to improve?</u> <u>How will I make the Current Self-Concept more like my Perfect Self?</u>: *I will tell myself to speak up when I have something to say. I matter.*

Difference #1: _positive_

How to improve? _Restate my negative thought to make it positive_

Difference #2: _Fearless_

How to improve? _Try to throw my skills despite nervs_

Difference #3: _patience_

How to improve? _Things take time repeat that to myself_

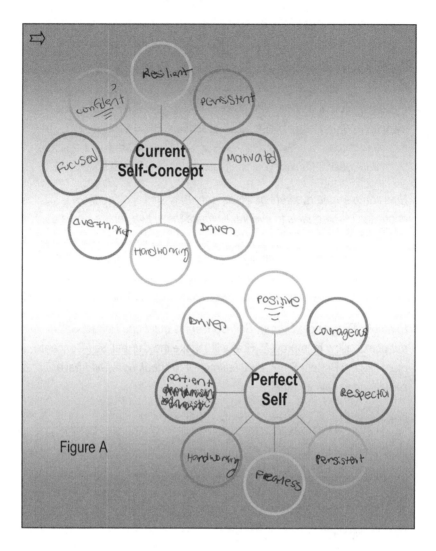

Figure A

Courage

Courage is a unique type of confidence. I see it as a combination of complete confidence and zero confidence. Initially you lack confidence, then cover it up with overconfidence, and end up with confidence. The ability to turn it around, to take a difficult situation and make it work in your favor is very useful and productive. Courage can come in handy when you are performing a risky skill, feeling overly nervous, mentally or physically tired, or facing an intimidating opponent.

Becoming courageous is a decision. You must stand up to your fears and decide that you will no longer be controlled by them. Start NOW. Do something today that you were afraid to do last week. Eventually you'll stop living with limits you've placed on yourself. Next time you feel fearful, acknowledge the fear, take a deep breath, and go forward with courage. Don't look back. Think how you will feel after you accomplish whatever you were fearful of. Think of how much your confidence will increase. Keep that feeling in your mind and step forward confidently.

> *"Courage is not the absence of fear, but rather the judgment that something else is more important than fear."*
> *—Ambrose Redmoon*

Confidence Building Strategies

There are many ways to boost your confidence. To avoid being overwhelmed by the wide selection of strategies, choose one strategy from each of the four categories: stay positive, celebrate success, take it easy on yourself, and get inspired. In the next few weeks, choose a different one from each category. Like the Buffet Rule states, eventually try everything at least once, then just stick to your top 3-5 techniques. Keep an open mind and give each strategy a genuine try, you may be surprised by what works for you.

1. Stay Positive
A. Embrace a Positive Philosophy
Make up a motto for yourself that empowers and motivates you to succeed. It is important that it is meaningful to you. Examples are "Rock Beam in 2018", "Nothing is impossible", "Dream Big", "No fear this year", "Expect more, get more", "I can and I will", "I am awesome", or "Screw it, just do it." Post it in your locker, gym bag, your mirror, or closet door; somewhere that you'll see it daily. Each time you see it, say it proudly.

B. Positive Encouragement

Do not underestimate the power of positive thought. The mind can be "tricked" into thinking whatever we want it to think. You probably do this daily with justifying negative behavior. "It's ok if I study for my test tomorrow, even though the test is the next morning. I'll have enough time," or "It's ok if I skip gymnastics and hang out with my friends instead. I'll just work out twice as hard tomorrow." This also works well when tricking your mind to think positively or be a confident athlete. You may have heard of the age old "fake it 'til you make it."

ACTIVITY

Write down a positive statement on an index card. It can be any sentence that makes you feel good about yourself, or something that you wish were true about yourself. For example, "I got 3rd place at a huge meet when I was only 9", "I worked really hard and got my kip", or "I am a happy, confident, successful person" (even if you aren't completely happy, confident, or successful). Think of any great accomplishments, compliments, proud moments, or something even as simple as "I am awesome." Remember, this is something that makes you feel proud of yourself, no one has to know what it is. Say this statement to yourself at least 5 times a day.

C. Thought Stopping

When a negative thought creeps into your head, it tends to stick around and progress into something worse. The best way to fix this is to stop it immediately before it has time to infect your mind.

1. The first step is becoming more aware of your thoughts. Make it a point to listen to what you say to yourself. At first, just recognize when you are thinking negatively or positively.

2. The next step is to stop the thought in its tracks. You can think of a big red STOP sign (you can use an actual picture of it if you're struggling with a clear picture), say stop out loud (when it's

appropriate), snap your fingers, lightly tap your leg, abruptly shake your head as if shaking the thought out of your mind, or wear a rubberband or hair-tie and snap it gently when you think negatively.

3. The third step is to replace the "problem" thought with a "productive" thought. In this case, something positive. It should be related to the negative thought but also believable. For example, if you think "I can't believe I missed that landing, I suck!" picture a big STOP sign, and then replace it with, "No one is perfect, I was a little distracted so I will focus on sticking next time and dig my toes into the mat."

D. Best Friend Test
When you make a mistake, you may say some pretty awful things to yourself. But if your best friend made the same mistake, would you say that to them? I would hope not. Next time you make a mistake, say to yourself what you say to your best friend. Most likely, it will be more productive than a scolding from yourself.

2. Celebrate Success
A. Imagine Perfection
Imagine yourself performing perfectly. This doesn't have to be an actual performance, it can be an imaginary ideal performance that you wish would happen. If you can see it in your head, you are more likely you will believe it can happen, and more likely to try it.

B. Success List
Think of all of your past successes. Think of your biggest achievements, greatest efforts, positive attributes, characteristics, and anything that makes you proud of yourself. Write down a list of these. As long as it makes you proud, write it down! One by one remember everything about that specific success. Think mostly about how it felt, but also what you heard, saw, touched, smelled, and even tasted, and recreate it vividly in your mind. Focus on these successes when you're feeling low.

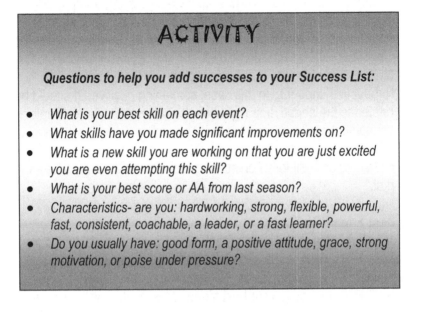

ACTIVITY

Questions to help you add successes to your Success List:

- *What is your best skill on each event?*
- *What skills have you made significant improvements on?*
- *What is a new skill you are working on that you are just excited you are even attempting this skill?*
- *What is your best score or AA from last season?*
- *Characteristics- are you: hardworking, strong, flexible, powerful, fast, consistent, coachable, a leader, or a fast learner?*
- *Do you usually have: good form, a positive attitude, grace, strong motivation, or poise under pressure?*

C. Tracking Progress

Seeing improvement and results is an automatic confidence boost. Track your progress so that you have physical evidence that you are actually improving. Make a chart, have a journal, or write it down somewhere. Don't forget to celebrate the small stuff too. New skills, a good effort, or improvements in mental skills are nothing to brush off lightly.

D. State of Mind and Body

Knowing that your mind and body are ready to go increases your beliefs in your skills and allows you to be more confident. To assure your mind is ready for a performance, leave all emotional baggage at the door. Literally stand at the door and take a few seconds to leave it all behind if you need to. Don't go in the door until you're ready. This may take more than a few seconds in the beginning, so arrive early to practice if you think it will be a problem. If you're seriously stressing, check out the anxiety management chapter for ways to reduce anxiety. To make sure your body is ready for action, you need to put in more effort than the average athlete. You are a *gymnast* and have committed yourself to success. This means eating healthy, staying hydrated, sleeping enough at night, staying on top of your schoolwork to minimize stress, and using the mental skills you learn in this book.

3. Take it Easy on Yourself
A. Break it Down
Break down difficult tasks into smaller, more manageable parts. Doing an entire skill all at once may be overwhelming. Only adding one piece at a time **allows your confidence to build**.

- For connections or routines, perform the skills one at a time before connecting them all together. Move on to a slight pause in between, and then the final step is to get rid of the pause.
- Start with an easier skill altogether and work up to the more difficult one. Jumping right in with a difficult skill can be intimidating, but after trying a similar, but easier skill will build your confidence. For example: if you are having trouble tumbling, perform a tumbling series that is easy for you, maybe a back layout before you start twisting.
- Drill the different parts of one skill. You may need to ask your coach how to go about this one. For example, a backwalkover on beam: drill the reach back to the beam, drill the bridge, drill the handstand out of the walkover with a strong finish. Put them all together for a confident backwalkover.

B. Put it in Perspective
Don't let a bad performance crush your confidence. Put it into a *different* perspective. Sometimes a bad warm up or bad first try is just getting the kinks out, it is not the start of an hour of bad performances. Give yourself a break. Also try putting it into an *overall* perspective. Ask yourself is, "Will this matter in 5 years?" The answer is most likely no, so drop it and move on. However, if you think it will matter, then ask yourself, "Is this the worst thing happening to someone in the world right now?" The world will not end because you made a mistake or are having trouble going for a skill. Remind yourself to stop being stuck on mistakes and to move toward success with your next attempt.

C. Attributions
There are 4 things people attribute success and failure to: ability, effort, luck and task difficulty. When you succeed, don't blame it on good luck or an easy task- attribute it to your ability to succeed and you putting in the effort. Celebrate that! When you fail, don't blame it on your lack of ability- it could have been a difficult task, just bad luck, or you may not have put in enough effort (which can change). Be more aware of how you explain

your successes and "failures", and make changes to your explanations if you are being too hard on yourself.

4. Get Inspired
A. Similar Experience
Watching someone in a similar situation can help you see that the skill is indeed possible, and helps you visualize exactly how to do it. If a teammate can do a skill that you are struggling with, don't let jealousy take over- use them to your advantage. Watch their movements and burn those into your memory. Take a few moments daily and visualize those movements, and eventually see yourself doing the skill. Soon enough you'll have the confidence to complete the skill perfectly.

B. Watch the Pros
Watching your favorite elite gymnast or Olympian can increase motivation and confidence in your own skills. Seeing or imagining it makes you want to do it too and you'll start thinking, "If they can do it, why can't I?" You'll feel like a 5 year old who can't wait to just get out and practice. There is always a great increase in gymnastics immediately after the Olympics. Usually seeing someone perform amazing feats or winning a gold medal makes you believe you could too if you just worked harder.

C. Uplifting Book or Movie
Read an uplifting book or watch an inspiring movie, either gymnastics-related, sport-related or even totally unrelated. Watching something inspiring but unrelated to your sport can still be inspiring and make you feel like you can do anything!

D. Friend and Family Support
Support from family and friends will increase your confidence and inspiration. A few words of encouragement can go a long way. Don't expect people to come to you, so seek out support from loved ones. Ask them one simple question: "Do you believe in me?" Their response may surprise and humble you.

Pre-Performance Routine

Having a usual routine before a competition creates familiarity and comfort.. and confidence! Reviewing from chapter 3, your PPR will be used in multiple occasions: before competitions, before each competitive event, before routines in practice, and before difficult skills. Your pre-meet PPR may involve listening to music, talking to teammates or family, stretching, visualizing, reciting a favorite inspirational quote, doing a team cheer, reading, or journaling. Immediately before your routines or difficult skills should be a quick review of your mental toughness skills. Whatever you do, make it consistent so it becomes comforting and builds your confidence. Remember to follow the guidelines from chapter 3 for pre-performance routines: *keep it short, keep it consistent and comforting, and avoid uncontrollable superstitions.*

We will be adding a step to your PPR in each chapter, and by the end of the book you will have a complete pre-performance routine. The first step is confidence. Start with your favorite confidence building strategy, the one you feel would give you the best confidence boost.

1. Confidence building technique: _____

CHAPTER 5
MOTIVATION

In This Chapter

- Benefits of Motivation
- Perseverance
- Commitment
- Right Theory of Motivation and Effort
- Pre-Performance Routine

Benefits of Being a Highly Motivated Gymnast

- Increased determination
- Increased intensity of effort
- Increased confidence
- Set and achieve more difficult goals
- Willingness to improve other mental skills

Perseverance

Being an unstoppable gymnast means that you cannot be stopped, and perseverance is not stopping until you have succeeded. Therefore you can guess that perseverance is a skill that is absolutely required to become unstoppable. This however is <u>not</u> the "never give up" pep talk you've heard before. You can't just be satisfied with the fact that you didn't quit. #notimpressed. Quitting shouldn't even be a thought that crossed your mind. You need to push your limits every day, going until you reach your breaking point and then going further.

Redefine "Hard Work"
Everyone has a different definition of what "hard work" is. Take a look at the Borg RPE (Rating of Perceived Exertion) Scale (Borg, 1998) below and keep in mind that exertion is another word for effort:

Exertion	RPE
No exertion at all	6
Extremely light	7
	8
Very light	9
	10
Light	11
	12
Somewhat hard	13
	14
Hard	15
	16
Very hard	17
	18
Extremely hard	19
Maximal exertion	20

Figure B

These are subjective ratings of how hard you are working. In order to increase your level of perseverance you need to redefine what these ratings mean to you. Say you and an out-of-shape friend were to work at a level of "very hard" on a treadmill. You would be going faster than them because a speed that is "very hard" for them may be just "somewhat hard" for you. Your objective is to increase your level of effort and pain tolerance while lowering the RPE. Meaning, raise your standards; what is "very hard" for you now should turn into just "hard" after time. This is the idea of playing through pain, but I do not condone playing through injuries, don't be stupid. Be gymnast tough, but don't hurt yourself!

Determination Through Meaning

> "You can measure a man's greatness by how much it takes to discourage him."
> -Robert G. Savage

When it is snowing outside and you have a super comfortable bed, will you still be determined to put in an extra morning practice? When your legs feel like bricks, will you be motivated to run up one more flight of stairs? When you are so frustrated because you cannot obtain a difficult skill, will you give up or will you push through? An intense determination is required to put in the extra effort and is required to become unstoppable. If simply getting out of bed is going to stop you, you cannot expect to be an unstoppable gymnast.

ACTIVITY

Answer these questions for yourself: *Why are you here? Why did you get out of bed? What makes you give full effort at practice? What do you want out of yourself today, tomorrow, and in 5 years? Why do you do gymnastics?* _____

_____

_____

When you sit down and decide what it is that you really want, you give gymnastics meaning and your efforts have more **direction and purpose**. *You have something to work for and something to focus on, resulting in an increased determination.* ⇨

⇨   Get a vision in your head of whatever the answer is to these questions: making it to level 10, competing in college, coming in 1st at your biggest meet of the year, gaining new incredible skills, etc. Use your visualizing skills and recreate this vision in your mind with full detail using all your senses. Think of a word or phrase to wrap up this image.

Yell this word as loud as you can! (if the situation allows it- yell into a pillow, in the shower, in your car, or with teammates). Say this word to yourself when you need to persevere and push through a difficult time.

What's your word? _____

One More

Most gymnasts are talented, and most work hard too. What's going to make you different? Well one, your mental skills that you have learned in this book. But also working *harder* than everyone else. If you were to brag to someone about your skills (PS. don't), would you be able to back it up with your work ethic and actions? If you want to be unstoppable, you need to do more than the rest. You need to do *one more* than everyone else; one more drill, one more set of pushups, one more lap. Use the "one more rule" in practice. When you have reached the required amount of drills, do one more. Once you reach your breaking point, do one more.

> "The vision of a champion is someone who is bent over, drenched in sweat, at the point of exhaustion, when no one else is looking." -Anson Dorrance

Commitment

Are you fully committed to being a gymnast? You probably answered yes pretty quickly. However, take some time and honestly evaluate your commitment. A full commitment involves making social, physical, and mental sacrifices for gymnastics, keeping your mind and body at a healthy athletic level at all times, and following all rules set in place by your team. Commitment and motivation go hand in hand. If you are fully committed you have no choice but to go for it 100%. Jumping off a cliff requires full commitment. You can't give 50% commitment and only fall 50%. If you commit to jumping, you commit to the whole fall. If you commit to your sport, you commit to everything it requires, the good and the bad; the successes and the sacrifices. Once you sit down and decide to fully commit to your sport, motivation will follow naturally. Make a contract for yourself with specific commitments you will make. This will compel you to stay committed and motivated.

Right Theory of Motivation and Effort

This is a theory that I developed and I must say it is definitely right! You will start at the left side with your initial level of effort, and move on to each consecutive step as you "make it right" to increase your motivation and effort. In order to increase *long-term* motivation and effort, you must start with the right environment and move onto the next step in order. You will find that skipping a step may increase short-term motivation, but it will come back to haunt you. You will not be able to maintain your new increased level of motivation or effort, and you will eventually fall back to the skipped step and still need to make it right.

Julie's Right Theory of Motivation and Effort

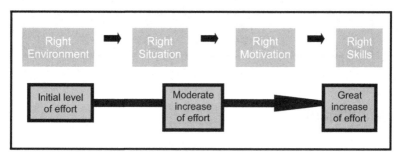

Figure C

1. Right Environment

Your environment consists of the people and places that you see on a daily basis. This usually includes your home, work, school, and teammates. The environment you are in affects your attitude and ultimately your motivation and effort. It should be an environment that makes you *want* to work hard. Personally, I need a positive and supportive environment to make me work hard. If I am yelled at, it makes me want to stop what I'm doing and curl up in a ball in a corner. For other people, a kick in the butt is just what they need. They need someone to not put up with their crap, and tell them exactly what they need to do, and to do it NOW.

Decide what type of environment is the best for you, and communicate to others about this. People are not mind readers. Tell people if you need more support. Tell people if you need them to be tough with you. Let them know what you need, and if possible, only look to the people willing to help you.

2. Right Situation

Gymnasts are either motivated by self-improvement or competition. Sometimes you are some of both, but there should be one that you are more like than the other. Which one are you? There are no wrong answers!

a. Self-Improvement

This gymnast is motivated by perfecting skills during practice, obtaining new skills, and improvements in event and All Around scores. These gymnasts are more persistent in their efforts to achieve progress during times of struggle, and through mistakes and failure. It makes them mad when they mess up and try even harder the next time until they get it just right. They will feel great accomplishment and pride when they succeed in their efforts to improve upon their performance.

b. Competition

This gymnast is motivated by comparisons of achievements with others. These gymnasts feel accomplishment in defeating others at meets, in-practice contests (handstand contest, conditioning contests, who can stick the most landings, etc.), the results of the competition, or any sort of evaluation of effort. These gymnasts are more persistent to succeed when others are watching. Simply by having others there, either observing or participating, these gymnasts will be more persistent and will feel great pride when coming in first.

Changing a Situation to Self-Improvement
You can do things for yourself to add more focus on self-improvement. Set goals and track your progress on drills, skills, and conditioning. Keep a journal to write down when you learn new things or get a personal best (number of pushups, number of repetitions completed in a drill, etc.), and soon you'll have a long list of improvements to be proud of.

Changing a Situation to Competitive
Chances are there is someone else on your team who is just as competitive as you are. Work out with them and push each other. Team up during paired drills and make it a competition. Also, learn to compete against yourself. Instead of beating opponents, beat your own records. Compete against your last performance, or the "you" from last year. Be faster, stronger, quicker, *better.*

3. Right Motivation
Which of these is most motivating to you? Again, there are no wrong answers!
1. Someone saying, "You'll never do that, that's too hard!"
2. Having a picture of you doing gymnastics on your team's social media page
3. Someone pulling you aside and saying, "You've been working really hard. I appreciate your effort and I'm proud of you!"
4. Doing each skill perfectly and taking pride in improvements

Option #1:
If you were most motivated by #1, then you like a challenge. You love to prove people wrong, and work twice as hard to do it. Challenge yourself by setting tough goals. The more difficult it is, the harder you'll work to prove you can do anything. Make your motto (from the confidence chapter) something to do with challenges, such as "prove 'em wrong" or "nothing is impossible." Also, follow in Michael Phelps' footsteps and make a bulletin board. Every time someone said something negative about him, he put the newspaper article up on his board and it fueled him

to work harder. Whenever an unsupportive coach, friend, or family member says something negative or acts unsupportive, write their words or actions down and post it. Turn the negativity into motivation to prove them wrong.

Option #2:
If you were most motivated by #2, then you like recognition. When someone recognizes you for your success or hard work, take pride in that. However, you can't force others to recognize you, and you can't solely depend on others for your motivation. Create your own "hall of fame" by making a bulletin board. Post all evidence of your success such as pictures, articles, medals, or note cards with the name of a new skill you learned or your highest AA from last year, for example.

Option #3:
If you were most motivated by #3, then you like appreciation. First off, make sure you are always working hard and focusing on the task to give your coach the opportunity to appreciate your effort. (If you aren't working hard, then you are missing an opportunity to be appreciated!) Make a goal *(next chapter!)* to work at 100% effort at your next practice. Second, just like recognition, appreciation cannot be forced. Increase your chances of being appreciated by working hard, being a good person, and appreciating your friends, family, and teammates with genuine thank-yous and kind words; you should receive some appreciation in return.

Option #4:
If you were most motivated by #4, then you like quality. Don't cut corners, do everything to your best ability, and don't except anything less than that. You are a perfectionist, so aim high. Straight legs, pointed toes, stuck landings, and nothing less. Keep practicing until you have a skill down. When you do achieve a quality performance, take pride in that. Have a journal and write down the skill and date of your quality achievements. Soon you'll have written proof of your greatness to be motivated by.

4. Right Skills
The last step is having the right skills to continue to motivate yourself to get to the next level. These are the other skills in your MTP. Since all sport psychology skills are connected, increasing your confidence, commitment to goals, visualizing success, managing anxiety, and

increasing your focusing skills, will also increase your motivation. Continue developing these skills as you continue your gymnastics career. Once you make it to this last step, you simply need to maintain this high level of motivation by keeping your skills sharp. Also, be aware that your environment and team objective may change as you move up levels and change coaches and teammates. A compulsory level is very different from an optional level team, so you will need to go back and make each step right again.

Pre-Performance

Step 2 of your pre-performance routine is to add your answer to the motivation question: *Why do you do gymnastics?* This will remind you of what you are working towards and exactly why you should give full effort in the moment.

1. Confidence building technique: _____

2. Motivation purpose: _____

CHAPTER 6
GOAL SETTING

In This Chapter

- Benefits of Setting Goals
- Types of Goals
- The Goal Setting Process: The Starting Line, Journey, and Destination
- Goal Setting Obstacles
- Pre-Performance Routine

Benefits of Setting Goals

> *"If you don't know where you're going, you'll probably end up someplace else."*
> -Yogi Berra

When you sit down and decide what it is that you really want, you give gymnastics more meaning, and your efforts have more direction and purpose. You have something to work for and something to focus on, resulting in an increased effort, persistence, and intensity. Plus, once you achieve your goal, you have a feeling of accomplishment and your confidence is boosted. If that isn't enough for you, the sport psychology research strongly supports the use of goal setting. In a review of over 500 studies on goal setting, 90% of the studies had positive results and for many, resulted in improvements in performance. Also, U.S. Olympic athletes use goal setting the most over any other mental skill. So if you want to be like Simone Biles, Aly Raisman, Nastia Liukin, Shawn Johnson, Carly Patterson, Nadia Comăneci, or any of your favorite Olympians or elite gymnasts, set yourself up on the right path using some simple goal setting techniques.

(Anderson, Crowell, Doman, & Howard, 1988; Brobst & Ward, 2002; Burton, 1983, 1989; Filby, Maynard, & Graydon, 1999; Gould, Tammen, Murphy, & May, 1989; Lambert, Moore, & Dixon, 1999; Locke, 1981; Swain & Jones, 1995; Orlick & Partington, 1988; Wanlin, Hrycaiko, Martin, and Mahon, 1997; Ward & Carnes, 2002; Weinberg, Stitcher, & Richardson, 1994). (Like I said, there is strong support for goal setting!)

Types of Goals

Alright, so let's get this thing started. What goals should you be setting? I say goal**s** because you need to set more than one goal. You will lose motivation if you try to focus on one goal for so long. So instead of a steep, slippery slope to climb to get to the top, you will have steps to help get you there (Figure D).

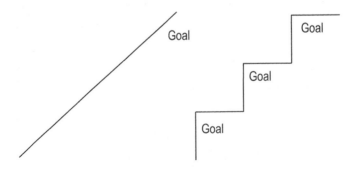

Figure D

Short-Term, Intermediate, and Long-Term Goals

In order to be an unstoppable gymnast, you need to be motivated and focused **all season long**. Term goals will help with that as they are spread out all throughout the year. You will be setting one of each of these (Figure E).

Short-term goals are meant to be achieved within a week to a couple months, so the difficulty level should be set accordingly. These are good for getting motivated in the short-term (hence the name). For now you will be setting one short-term goal, but as you become more comfortable with the goal setting process, you may set more than one short-term goal (see Figure F). The short-term goal should be a step towards achieving the intermediate and long-term goals.

Intermediate goals are meant to be achieved within a couple months to a year. The intermediate goal should also be a step towards achieving the long-term goal. Just like the short-term goals, you will set one of these for now, and progress to two as you become more familiar with the goal setting process.

Long-term goals should be the highest difficulty level and should take at least 6 months to several years. The long-term goal is what you want to achieve in the end. You could define "the end" as the end of the season, or even the end of your career; it's up to you to decide the time-frame of your goals. You should ideally only set one long-term goal at a time.

Outcome, Performance, and Process Goals

These types of goals focus on the *topic* of your goal. You will be setting a mixture of these, but ideally mostly process goals.

Outcome goals focus on the result of a meet. This would be winning first AA, earning a trophy or qualifying for finals. These goals are not just based on *your* efforts, but *your opponent's* efforts as well. Many uncontrollable factors come into play when focusing on winning. Your success depends on judges' scores, opponents, teammates, and sometimes a little bit of luck. You may have had the best meet of your life, but because someone else did too, you didn't achieve your goal. For these reasons, you should only set one outcome goal at a time. These goals aren't all bad though, and let's face it- gymnasts are driven by winning. It's hard not to dream about winning the highest title your level offers. Outcome goals facilitate short-term motivation, and increase motivation and effort in the moment. So as long as you set the other types of goals, the outcome goal is truly motivating and a great pre-competition pep-talk topic.

Performance goals focus on improving upon one's own performance. These goals could involve getting a better score on bars, getting a new skill, or sticking a beam routine. Unlike the outcome goal, these goals are generally based on *your* efforts alone. They are good for increasing effort level and attention to problem areas. Making too many mistakes on beam? Make it a goal to increase your beam score, and most likely you'll spend some more time perfecting your beam routine.

Process goals focus on performing with correct physical or mental skill technique. These goals are the best for improving performance because they hit the root of the problem: technique. Examples of process goals could be keeping pointed toes in a leap, staying hollow in a back layout, or sticking a certain percentage of your landings. Process goals are based *solely* on your efforts, which is ideal. Research shows that setting process goals is the most effective form of goal setting and facilitates long-term motivation. Where winning the state championship all-around will motivate you immediately, process goals are an on-going motivational tool. When you aren't so psyched to be at practice, you can at least stay motivated to work on your process goal.

Practice and Competition Goals

You may only focus on doing well in competitions, however <u>how</u> do you perform well in a competition? *By practicing well.* If you set goals for practice, you will increase the quality of your practice and in turn increase the quality of your competition performance. Only perfect practice makes perfect. You should set a mixture of practice and competition goals.

Daily and Weekly Goals

These are optional goals, and should only be used once you are comfortable with the goal setting process. The only caution is to not overwhelm yourself with too many goals. Daily goals are small goals set each day. Ask yourself, "What do I want out of practice today?" It should be something simple and easy to achieve. A daily goal could be, "I will do at least 10 tumbling passes with good form," or "I will say 5 positive things about myself today." Weekly goals are just that; small goals for the week. If you want to get fancy, you could set an easier, attainable goal for the week and a harder one that you'll really have to work hard to achieve. This way you'll feel a sense of accomplishment out of every week, and really great on the weeks you achieve the harder goal.

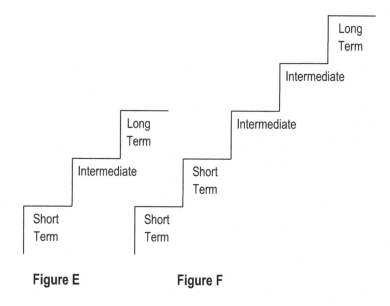

Figure E   **Figure F**

The Goal Setting Process: The Starting Line

The goal setting process is like a race. At the beginning, the starting line, you need to set things up and prepare for the race. You should decide the topic of your goals, deadlines, and how you are going to reach these goals. The first four steps of goal setting are at the starting line before you've even begun.

1. Establish a long-term goal
2. Set short-term and intermediate goals that will help you get to the long-term goal
3. Create specific goal achievement strategies for <u>how</u> each goal will be achieved
4. Set a deadline (and reward only if needed) for each goal

Topic and Guidelines

Keeping the different types of goals in mind, the topic of your goal is unlimited. Some ideas are:

- improving technique
- acquiring a new skill
- improving flexibility or strength
- increasing enjoyment
- improving a score or AA
- increasing effort level

- moving up a level
- sticking a routine
- qualifying for finals/nationals
- improving mental skills
- increasing confidence
- winning 1st place

The best way to determine the topics of your goals is to honestly answer the question, "At the end of the season, what would I be most proud to say I achieved?" While you have full power to choose your goals, you still need to follow some guidelines to make your goal effective. This is what I call setting "SPICY" goals.

SPICY Goals:

- **S**pecific- Be precise in what you want to achieve. You will be more focused on achieving something specific rather than a goal of "getting better at vaulting."
- **S**everal- Set a variety of goals so that you're not bored and can keep your motivation going. Set all types of goals: long-term, short-term, outcome, performance, process, practice, competition, etc.
- **P**ositive terms- Set goals using positive wording. Having a goal of "not making mistakes" or "not falling off beam," brings your attention to the mistakes, not what you need to do to succeed.
- **I**n measurable terms- You need to be able to measure whether you have achieved your goal or not. "10 flight series stuck on beam," can be measured, while "improving my flight series," is more difficult

to measure. For concepts like confidence or anxiety level, you can use a rating system of 1-10 on how you feel.

- **C**hallenging- Make it moderately difficult. A realistic difficulty level, but challenging enough to make you work hard for it. Too easy and you'll be bored; too hard and you risk giving up.
- **C**ontrollable factors- Make most of your goals within your control. Remember you don't have too much control over how you place or whether you get a trophy. Keep most of your goals as process and performance goals.
- **Y**our own- Make it personal and meaningful. Don't let your coach or teammates set a goal for you. Like we discussed in the last chapter, you need to be extremely motivated and determined, and a goal with little meaning to you won't be motivating in the long run.

Goal Achievement Strategies

Once you set your goal, you need to establish exactly how you plan to achieve it. For example, if your short-term goal is to "Get my backhandspring," in the next month, how are you going to make that happen? You can't just hope that it happens without any practice, conditioning, or drills. You could say to achieve this goal I will devote 10 additional minutes every practice to working on backhandspring drills, and I will ask my coach for feedback on how to improve my form.

Deadlines and Rewards

A set deadline creates a sense of urgency to achieve the goal, and reduces procrastination. It should be a realistic deadline, giving you enough time to achieve it while still making you work for it; not too soon, not too late. Rewards can be set for each goal, however, set them *carefully.* ***Achieving the goal should be the reward itself.*** That feeling of accomplishment should be the best feeling ever! However, you know yourself best, and if you know that you'll need something extra to push you to get there, then go ahead. These should not interfere with achieving your later goals. For example, a day off from a scheduled practice isn't a good reward because it takes away from future progress.

The Goal Setting Process: The Journey

Now that you have completed the first four steps in the goal setting process at the starting line, continue with the next steps in the journey:

5. Start working towards your short-term goal and track your progress (use the chart in the Appendix)
6. Achieving your goal- If you achieve your goal before your deadline, celebrate your success and move on to the next goal! If you missed the deadline, either adjust the deadline to give yourself more time, or adjust the difficulty of the goal.

Track Your Progress

Track your progress by writing your goals somewhere- use the chart in the Appendix, write them in a journal, on a calendar, or on an index card that you can keep in your gym bag. Display your goals somewhere that is visible to you daily so you always know what you're working towards.

Obstacles

If you knew there was a giant pothole up ahead on the road, wouldn't you make a plan to go around it? Same thing here. Potential obstacles and excuses should be identified to eliminate surprises and reduce the risk of giving up on the goal setting process (Gentner, 2007). The top problems are:

- Frustration
- Lack of motivation
- Lack of time
- Lack of confidence
- Feeling lost or confused
- Feeling overwhelmed

ACTIVITY

1. Identify specific problems you may encounter on the way to reaching your goal. What excuses do you usually use? What problem would cause you to be distracted from your goal?

2. Think of ways to prevent these problems from happening or coping strategies for if they do occur. Make a prevention plan for yourself and write it here or in a journal. (see Obstacles section on previous page)

1. Usual Excuses: ⟹ *Prevention Plan:*

_____ ⟹ _____

_____ _____

2. Potential Problems: *Prevention Plan:*

_____ ⟹ _____

_____ ⟹ _____

Suggestions for Goal Success

Be flexible. If you miss a part of a goal, don't give up on the whole thing. If you planned to work on a skill Monday, Wednesday, and Friday, and don't do it on Wednesday, don't just give up on Friday. Change it to 3 times a week so you can stay flexible with which days you work on the skill.

Get support. Have a support system intact for those times where you are too tired or frustrated to keep going. A few words of encouragement from a friend can go a long way. Involve your coach as well so they can help you along the way with technique, feedback, or pushing you to give extra effort. Make sure your coach knows your motivation type (previous chapter).

Commit to the goal. The goal setting chart in the Appendix has a spot for you and a witness to sign as if it is a contract. Making it public to your family, friends, coach, and/or teammates puts the idea out there that if you don't keep at it, others will know. Follow through with what you started!

Modify your goals. If you do hit an obstacle, keep in mind that goals aren't set in stone. Don't be too lenient and let yourself off the hook too quick, but don't let yourself get so frustrated that you want to quit either. Reset goals that just aren't working, cut back and focus only on the most important goals, modify the deadline, modify the difficulty level, make it more personal and meaningful, make them "spicy", and/or modify your schedule to make time for your goals.

The Goal Setting Process: The Destination

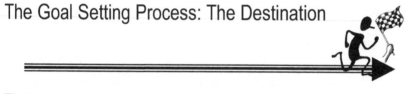

The last step in the goal setting process:

7. Keep going until you reach your long term goal. Celebrate your success and then start the journey over again with new goals!

CONGRATS! Celebrate the achievement of your goal! You have just achieved something GREAT, so be proud of your success and allow your confidence to grow! However, now the destination becomes the starting point. Set your sights higher and set new goals. Never be satisfied with being mediocre. Gymnastics is about always improving yourself, so continue to strive to be the best. Let your new goals reflect that.

Goal Setting Chart

Use the goal setting chart in the Appendix and the knowledge you've just learned to set effective goals. I suggest using the 3 goal chart first, and then the 5 goal chart after you are comfortable with the goal process.

Putting all the steps together:
1. Establish a long-term goal
2. Set short-term and intermediate goals that will help you get to the long-term goal
3. Create specific goal achievement strategies for <u>how</u> each goal will be achieved
4. Set a deadline (and reward only if needed) for each goal
5. Start working towards your short-term goal and track your progress.
6. Achieving your goal- If you achieve your goal before your deadline, celebrate your success and move on to the next goal. If you missed the deadline, either adjust the deadline to give yourself more time, or adjust the difficulty of the goal.
7. Keep going until you reach your long-term goal. Celebrate your success and then start the journey over again with new goals!

Pre-Performance

Step 3 of your pre-performance routine is to remind yourself of your current goal. Focus on the actions needed for achievement. What are you supposed to be working on in this moment, on this day? A simple reminder will keep you focused on the task and increase your motivation and effort.

1. Confidence building technique: _____
2. Motivation purpose: _____
3. Reminder of goals: _____

CHAPTER 7
VISUALIZATION

In This Chapter

- Benefits of Visualization
- Defining Imagery and Visualization
- Visualization Principles
- Visualization Uses
- Effective Visualization
- Visualization Scripts
- Potential Challenges

Benefits of Visualization

- Develop skills to relax on cue
- Feel more confident in skills
- Be prepared for the expected and unexpected
- Manage stress more efficiently
- Recover from mistakes and adverse situations more effectively
- Improve performance over time

Visualization Defined

Visualization is the ability to control thoughts, feelings, emotions, attention, and images in a passive manner. Think of it as a dream you are trying to control. The terms "visualization" and "imagery" are commonly used interchangeably but actually have different meanings. I will primarily be using the term visualization to cover both variations just to attempt to simplify things. Visualization is purely visual- a silent movie in HD, while imagery is the use of all senses- a 4D movie with surround sound. While imagery sounds like the better choice, each has their advantages and uses. Imagery is best for preparation and coping since a more realistic image will help prepare you for the real thing. Visualization, pure vision, is the way to go when you are trying to improve or change a skill. You don't need all the distractions of sound, smell, or touch. You just need to see the movement and nothing else, so just a visual picture is more effective.

Visualization Principles

Visualization may be seen as one of the more "touch-feely" skills. Many athletes like to be seen as tough, and closing your eyes and seeing pictures in your head may not fit that image. However, without the ability to see yourself succeed in your mind, you won't be able to do it in reality. To prove to you that this is beneficial, here are two principles for you to consider:

1. The Imagination Principle (Shelley, 2007)
The Imagination Principle states that "the mind does not know the difference between what is real and what is imagined." A great example is the classic dream where you are falling. We have all sat straight up in bed, sweating, out of breath, and glad to realize it was a dream, and that we are not really falling 10,000 feet from a plane. However, your body responded to your thoughts as if it was real. Your mind thought you were falling and your body followed suit.

2. The Principle of Dominant Thought (Shelley, 2007)
This principle states that "whatever dominates my thoughts is what I move towards." Another classic example is demonstrated in the kitchen. Have you ever tried to put the milk away in the microwave? I have. I was thinking so much about heating up my food that that's where I moved towards: the microwave. It didn't matter that I had milk in my hand, not food; the microwave was dominating my thoughts. This principle translates into gymnastics through thinking about mistakes. Not going for your flyaway is dominating your thoughts, so guess what you do? Tight death grip on the bar and you don't go for your flyaway.

Visualization Uses

The unstoppable gymnast will use visualization and imagery for relaxation, preparation, and coping. Visualization of relaxation uses calming images, deep breathing, and progressive muscle relaxation, all of which will be covered in detail in the next chapter, Anxiety Management.

Preparation
Using visualization for preparation will mentally rehearse the actions your body is about to take. This gets your mind and muscles focused on the skill or routine, and the image increases your confidence in your ability to execute the actions. If you can see it, you'll be more likely to be able to do it, which is why imagery (using all the senses) is best used for preparation. It is more helpful to imagine a competition setting, even if you are in practice, to prepare for an actual meet. This will help you deal with the nerves when you are at a real meet.

Mental preparation not only prepares your mind for your performance, but your muscles as well. To prove it, try the activity on the next page. Also, when mentally rehearsing, imagine yourself performing perfectly. Save the mistakes for the coping visualization. If you do make mistakes in your preparation, stop the image and start again. Take a break if you can't get it perfect, and come back to it at a different time.

Coping

Another use of visualization is coping. This means imagining an injury, mistakes or setbacks, pressure situations, or any worst-case scenario. It may seem counter-intuitive to imagine the bad things, but it takes the surprise out of unexpected situations. This gives you the opportunity to think of a Plan A and Plan B in case it does happen. This is where the unstoppable gymnast can shine. An unexpected situation can make a normal gymnast crumble, where a mentally tough gymnast is unaffected and simply goes on to their Plan B.

For coping visualizations, imagine a mistake or negative situation, and then imagine recovering well from it. This allows you to practice Plan B without actually having to make the mistakes. Since we are going for vivid and realistic here, use all of your senses when imagining. For an injury, you could imagine yourself recovering and healing. You can be creative here, with an imaginary healing powder flowing through your veins to an injured leg and healing the ligaments, or the toxins exploding in black puffs and leaving your injured arm.

Effective Visualization

There are 5 key components for effective visualization:

- Location
- Vividness
- Controllability
- Perspective
- Focus

Location

Find someplace where you feel comfortable. Visualize at home or find a secluded part of the gym or locker room. Close your eyes and put your head down. Start with short visualization sessions of just a minute and work up towards 6 or 7 minutes. If you don't feel completely comfortable, the visualization will be interrupted by thoughts of, "Is anyone looking at me?" or "What's going on around me?" Once you feel comfortable visualizing in front of others, you can start visualizing during practice or a competition. Locations during a meet will most likely be sitting alone off to the side of the gym or sitting with your team with your head down while you wait for your turn or for others to finish while you think about your next event. At the very least, you only need a moment to take a deep breath or review or skill in your mind.

Vividness

The more vivid the image, the more effective it is in preparing you for the real thing. Use the activity to work on visualizing details and clear images. A vivid experience with full detail of sight, smell, sound, taste, and touch will make it more realistic and more believable that you can do the skill successfully. If you can see it, you can do it.

ACTIVITY

Imagine yourself standing in your kitchen. Make this image as vivid as you can... make it as if you were really there right now. Now imagine that you have a beautiful ripe lemon on the cutting board in front of you. Notice the bright yellow color. Pick the lemon up and feel the bumpy texture of the skin. Give it a little squeeze to feel that it is perfectly ripe. Now imagine putting the lemon back down on the ⇨

> ⇨ *cutting board. Pick up the knife and cut the lemon in half. As*
> *you cut notice the beads of lemon juice rolling down on to the cutting*
> *board. You can immediately smell the strong lemon scent. Now cut a*
> *small slice of the lemon. Pick up this juicy slice of lemon and imagine*
> *taking a nice big bite of this slice.* (Harrell, 2006)
>
> Were you able to taste the lemon at the end? Did your lips pucker at
> all? If not, keep practicing until you can actually taste the lemon!

Controllability

Controllability is imagining exactly what you want to imagine and being able to manipulate the imagined environment. This skill is important when imagining a performance without mistakes, and in the desired speed and direction. The speed should be in real time most of the time, but it could be beneficial to imagine a performance at a faster speed when preparing for a fast paced event like vault or a tumbling pass on floor. You could also visualize in a slower speed when starting to correct technique. The direction refers to the image going forwards, backwards, or paused. The direction will usually be forwards, however, it can go backwards if you make a mistake and want to go back to a previous point, without having to start the image all over. You can also use pause to look at one position in detail, which is helpful when learning a new skill or changing technique.

ACTIVITY

Imagine that you have a basketball, a baseball, and a soccer ball lined up on a table in front of you in that order from left to right- basketball, baseball, soccer ball. Pick up the basketball with your left hand. Toss it up gently in the air and catch it with your left hand. Hold it there. Now put the ball down on the right side of the balls. The order is now: baseball, soccer ball, basketball. Pick up the baseball with your right hand. Throw it up in the air and freeze it in midair. See it frozen in the air. Now rotate the ball as if it is on display for everyone to see. Put out your hands to catch the ball and let it fall into your hands when you are ready. Put the baseball back in its place. The order is still ⇨

> baseball, soccer ball, basketball. Put the soccer ball on the ground. Kick the ball and see it go far, far in the distance until you can't even see it anymore. Now reverse the direction of your imagery and see the ball come back to you from the distance, and land back in front of your foot. See yourself kick the ball again but in slow motion. Slowly you bring your foot back and slowly it kicks forward and hits the ball again. Now speed up the imagery and see the ball fly into the air and into the distance very quickly. Nice kick!

Perspective

The perspective in which you see the image can be external or internal. An external perspective is seeing yourself perform as a spectator would see it, or as if seeing yourself on video. An internal perspective is seeing yourself perform as you would see it through your own eyes. A mentally tough athlete needs both perspectives for different visualizations. An external perspective is useful for simply assessing how a skill looks and usually is just visual. Internal is most useful when changing technique or preparing for a performance, and usually uses all the senses. Try the activity below for practicing using the two perspectives.

ACTIVITY

Imagine that you are running on a track. See the track ahead of you with the lines on the black rubber. See the trees that outline the edge of the track, and the football goal posts at the end of the field. Look down and see your legs moving, one step at a time. Hear yourself breathing and heart pumping. Hear the other runners around you and the spectators clapping on the sidelines. Feel the wind against your skin. Clench and unclench your fists and feel the tension in your hands. Smell the hot dogs and nachos being sold at the concession stand as you run by it. Taste the saliva in your mouth as you continue to run harder. Now, as if you were looking through the lens of a camera, zoom out a little and watch yourself run.

⇨ *You no longer can touch, hear, taste, or smell, you can only see yourself moving from afar. Zoom out more. Watch the movements that you make as if you were watching from the bleachers of the stadium. One step after another; arms pumping, legs moving quickly.*

Zoom back in and go back into your body and see the world through your own eyes again for a moment. You can feel the wind, and hear the people. Now zoom back out to your place on the bleachers and watch yourself run.

For additional practice of the external perspective, review a video of yourself during a performance. Close your eyes for a few minutes and picture the video of yourself, then watch the video for a few minutes, and repeat. Gradually watch less of the video and more of your own vision. For additional practice of the internal perspective, take notice of everything around you right now. Vividly see the details of the objects and people currently near you. Close your eyes and recreate the image in front of you. Open your eyes and see how well you did. If you missed some things and imagined them differently, close your eyes again and see it perfectly. Try these exercises a couple times a day.

Focus
Eventually you need to work up to about 7 minutes for a single visualization session. Strong focus will be needed for maintaining an effective visualization for this long without mental interruptions. Whenever conflicting or intrusive thoughts interfere with the activity, stop visualizing. Deal with the interfering thoughts rather than trying to block them out. You may need to write down the thoughts that continue to bother you so you may concentrate on visualizing. After dealing with the thoughts, begin again. If the distracting thoughts occur again several times even after writing them down, stop the session and try to resolve the matter. Use the Stress List in the Appendix or try using the relaxation techniques in the next chapter and begin the session again when you are in a calmer state (Dorfman & Kuehl, 2002). However, eventually, an unstoppable gymnast will need to work through interfering thoughts and just focus on the skill or routine you are visualizing. This will take practice!

Visualization Scripts

Visualization scripts are written instructions for exactly what you want to imagine. Just like a movie script, you should read through the visualization script each time you visualize until you have it mostly memorized. They are very similar to the activities you have already done in this chapter, however, scripts focus on relaxation, preparation, or coping and are highly specific to you, your skills, and your routines. Again, the relaxation script will be discussed in the next chapter. You will be writing your own script, so you can use these as a base.

Preparation Script
Pick out a certain skill or routine that you want to mentally rehearse. Using all of your senses, experience your performance as best you can during a competition. Imagine what you would see through your own eyes. Imagine what you would hear, smell, and taste as if you were really performing. Imagine the feel of the movements as you perform it perfectly. Imagine and feel every single bend of the knee, twist of the neck, and extension of the elbow. If you are just learning this skill, you can slow down the vision just as you learned in the controllability section. If you are simply preparing for the skill, use real time. If you make a mistake during a skill or routine, stop the imagery immediately and either rewind the vision or start over until you see yourself performing perfectly.

Here is an example of a preparation script for a gymnast doing a front handspring on vault:

SCRIPT

Imagine yourself on the vault runway at a meet. Imagine the taste of fresh water as you take one more sip from your water bottle. Imagine the feeling of walking onto the blue fuzzy carpeting on your toes. Reach down and feel the shiny white measuring tape next to the runway. See your number on the measuring tape. Feel the sweat and a little bit of chalk on your hands as you rub them together. Look down the runway and see the cream colored springboard waiting for you to jump on it. See the tan leather vault table ready for your hands to launch you off of it. See your coach standing to the side, clapping their hands and encouraging you. Look at the judge in their blue blazer making final calculations from the previous gymnast. Listen to the murmur of the crowd as you get ready to vault. Hear your teammates as they cheer your name. See your coach as they motion to stay hollow and block in your vault. Taste the saliva in your mouth. Find your spot on the runway and feel your muscles move into ready position. See the small green flag wave at the judge's table, signaling it is time for you to vault. Feel your arms go up to present to the judge. Hear the sound of you breathing harder and your heart pumping. Hear your inner voice say "Go! You can do this, you rock!" Feel your muscles activate as you begin your powerful run and feel your toes dig into the runway, gaining speed with every step you take. Feel the wind against your arms as you pump them back and forth, still running faster. Hurdle onto the springboard and feel each of the springs compress and then give you power as they spring back up. Reach your arms up as high as you can, while you tighten your core muscles and drive your heels to the ceiling. Feel your hands connect to leather vault table briefly as your shoulders block off the table and send you into the air. Feel your shoulders squeeze your ears, core muscles squeeze to keep you hollow and your ankle bones glue together until you feel the landing mat on your feet where you bend your legs, dig your toes into the mat, and prepare your body for a stick position. Look at the blue mat around you and then face the judge for your finish. See their smiling face as they nod in approval. Listen to the sound of your teammates cheering and the crowding roaring your name!

Coping Script

For the coping script, you should imagine a worst-case scenario. You make a mistake at an important meet, you are at practice and your coach is pressuring you to do a skill you are terrified of, your team is behind and need your best routine to move into first place, you've already fallen off beam and do not want to fall again, it's your least favorite event up next, or on the next event you need to perform a skill you have not successfully landed in weeks. Whatever the scenario, it's your turn and need to perform better than you ever have before. Imagine in detail a worst-case scenario for you. Make several plans with positive outcomes, and visualize each one using all of your senses. Visualize recovering from adversity and performing perfectly.

Here is an example of a coping script for a situation where you are at a meet and need to perform a back full on floor, however, you have not completed it successfully at practice in several weeks:

SCRIPT

Imagine you are at a meet. See the other gymnasts in colorful leotards competing around you. Watch the judges gathering and settling in at their tables. Listen to the sounds of the crowd, teammates cheering for each other, and the coaches giving encouragement and corrections to their gymnasts. Smell the chalky air and the scent of freshly washed mats. Take a drink of water and taste the refreshing cool water as it hits your lips. Feel the fuzzy feeling of the floor exercise carpeting on your feet as you stand preparing to start your warm up. You haven't landed your back full in several weeks and are very worried about competing it, and actually have been stressing out about it for the last week. You tell yourself "I know I can do it. Trust yourself!" Hear a bell ring signifying the start of the warm up and a woman over the loud speaker saying "You may now begin your 2 minute touch." You start with some of your dance elements, leaps, jumps, and turns. You test out the bounciness of the floor. You warm up several handstands and standing backhandsprings off to the side. Feel your muscles flex as your legs stay straight and toes pointed in every skill. Walk to the corner as you begin your tumbling warm up. Look at the blue floor around you and white lines just at your feet. Hear the sounds of the floor creaking and springing as each gymnast tumbles, leaps, and lands each of their skills. You get into your ready position and tell yourself "Go!" You take off running, pumping your arms back and forth, using every muscle in your legs to get as much power as you can. You hurdle up tall and then reach out for your round off. You feel your body in the air, hands down on the ground, and blocking with your shoulders. Your feet land on the ground and immediately you are arching back for your backhandspring as you have a million other times. You push again, feet are landing again, reaching up and setting for your back layout. Feel yourself pull to the side with all of your arm strength, knowing exactly where you are in the air. Legs are straight, toes are pointed, core muscles engaged. You open up in a hollow body position and prepare to stick your landing. Feel your arms reach out forward, eyes up, and feet connect to the floor and don't move. "Let's do this," you say, "I am ready!" You are up first, so you walk off to the side of the floor and wait for warm up to end. The judge raises their hand and smiles, and you present with both arms up and a big smile back. See yourself get into your starting position and the start of your music. Feel your muscles begin your routine and dance and leap your way into the corner. Turn around and immediately start your powerful run into your back full. You do everything the same way you did in warm up- pumping arms, hurdling tall, reaching, blocking, staying tight. Feel the familiar motions, arms pull to the side with all you have and then feel your body opening up to your stick position and a solid landing. Finish your routine with confidence, a big smile, and a strong finish. You did it!

Write Your Own

Developing your own personal visualization script is more meaningful and useful. You can give much more detail about your surroundings and individual technique. First decide the purpose of your script- preparation or coping. Then start writing about your surroundings- what you see, how you feel, what you can hear. Describe the scenario of what you are dealing with, and then describe what you would want to happen with a positive outcome. Be creative, make it vivid and detailed, and don't be afraid to exaggerate a little.

Purpose: _____

Script: *Remember to include all senses, be VERY detailed about muscle movement, what you see, and how you feel.*

_____

_____

_____

_____

_____

_____

_____

_____

_____

_____

_____

_____

Potential Challenges

Not enough time during competition
For gymnastics, you *should* have enough time in between events to visualize. However, there will be times where you are last up or near the end of the rotation on one event, and first or near the beginning on the next event. So for these situations, you'll need quick mental preparation. You will need to practice a condensed version of your visualization script with only the key parts. You could also develop cue words, which will be discussed further in the focus chapter. At the very least, you only need a moment to take a deep breath, say a cue word, or review the most important skills in your mind.

Trouble focusing long enough
If you cannot focus long enough, start small and work up to longer time periods. Visualization is a skill to be practiced and mastered. It may not come easy at first. Start with 60 seconds and work up to about 6 or 7 minutes.

Trouble "seeing" yourself in your mind
If you cannot "see" yourself in your mind, use movement, floor music, your grips, or touching the equipment to help make the vision more clear. Actually put on your grips while visualizing your bar routine, put on your

floor music and go through the motions, sit on the beam while visualizing your beam routine, or put your arms in the air and simulate your rings routine with your arm movements.

Pre-Performance

Step 4 is to add visualization into your pre-performance routine. Pick either a preparation or coping script and summarize it below. Write your own script to use at home, and practice a condensed version for your pre-performance routine and/or during competition.

1. Confidence building technique: _____

2. Motivation purpose: _____

3. Reminder of goals: _____

4. Visualization (summarize your script with key parts): _____

_____

_____

CHAPTER 8
ANXIETY MANAGEMENT

In This Chapter

- Benefits of Anxiety Management
- Awareness
- Approach
- Assessment
- Pre-Performance Routine

Benefits of Anxiety Management

The benefits of being able to control your body and relax on cue are most definitely going to give you an advantage over your opponents. While their nerves are dominating their thoughts and negatively affecting their body, you can remain calm, cool, and collected and have a better overall performance. Control over your body allows your mind to rest and focus on the task. Since your body feels ready to go, your confidence increases in your ability to succeed. Continuous control of your body will result in more consistent performances, allowing you to improve on your skills, rather than fighting the battle of the nerves.

Awareness

When you become stressed, there is a *source* of that stress which causes *symptoms* of stress. It is useful to become more aware of both the source and symptoms to allow time to cope. Decide exactly what source causes you to be stressed out at a level that is more than you are able to handle- certain situations, people, or actions. For example, maybe out of all the events, you get *extra nervous* before beam. Or maybe there is one judge who never gives you good scores. Maybe you didn't land your tumbling pass in warm up. The first step is to have awareness of what sends you into a panic so that next time *you'll be able to do something about it* before you actually panic.

Next you should determine the *symptoms* of your stress. Sometimes you miss the source and you pass right into the symptoms before you even realize what happened. If you can catch your stress at the symptoms, there is still time to use a coping approach to help manage the anxiety. Generally, physical symptoms include increased heart rate, sweating, shaking, tense muscles, butterflies, and eventually sleep disturbances and fatigue. Mental symptoms of stress usually include negative or repetitive thoughts, irritability, frustration, and difficulty making decisions. After recognizing a source or symptom, use that as a cue to use one of the following coping approaches.

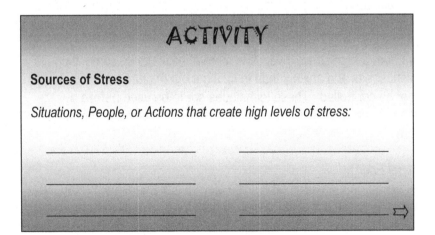

ACTIVITY

Sources of Stress

Situations, People, or Actions that create high levels of stress:

_____   _____

_____   _____

_____   _____ ⇨

⇨
Symptoms of Stress

Physical: *Mental:*

_____   _____

_____   _____

_____   _____

Approach

Different situations create different stressors, thus there are different approaches for lowering anxiety. You can use preventative coping, relaxation techniques, coping techniques, or psych-up techniques depending on the need. It is important to emphasize that feeling anxiety is inevitable- it is going to happen whether you like it or.. well, no one likes it, but it is unavoidable. The key to being unstoppable is not *avoiding* anxiety, but being able to *effectively deal with it*.

BEFORE: Preventative Coping
Let's back up a bit. Before you even get to practice or a meet, there are some things you can do to manage your stress and anxiety. It is easier to start at a low stress level and try to keep the level low than bring it back down from a high stress level. It is more effective to do some things to prevent stress and anxiety than to let it get out of hand where it can no longer be controlled. These techniques are to be used **before** a potentially stressful situation, either a few weeks beforehand or minutes before.

Optimal Energy
Energy can be measured on a scale of 1-10, 1 being almost sleep, 10 being on a sugar and caffeine high at the same time. Neither a 1 nor a 10 is optimal for athletic performance. You want to have some nerves to give you energy and an adrenaline rush. The optimal energy level (OEL) is

different for everyone, depending on personality and sport. A golfer doesn't need as much adrenaline as a football player. Also, a person who is normally more high-strung will probably have a higher OEL than someone who is more laid-back because that energy level is where they are most comfortable. A unique aspect of gymnastics is that the events are so different, you will have different OELs for each event. For the example below, we will say that 6 may be an optimal energy level for floor.

Energy Level

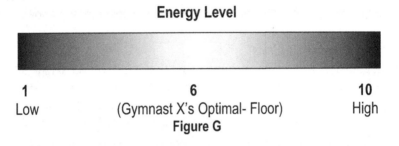

1	6	10
Low	(Gymnast X's Optimal- Floor)	High

Figure G

Most of the time you will need to lower your energy level to get to the OEL, which is many of the coping techniques are about learning to relax. However, sometimes you may find yourself at the lower end of the scale and will need to pump yourself up to get to the OEL.

Keep in mind, whether you are really happy or really upset, you are still at the high end of the OEL and not at the optimal level (Williams, 2005). Your body registers the increased heart rate, shakiness, and muscle tension as nerves. Your performance now may suffer because you are now in an altered physical state, even if it because you are super happy! After you become overly excited you would need to bring your energy level back down, which many gymnasts either struggle with or fail to do completely. Go into your competition knowing that it is great to be excited about your performance, your team's, or your teammates' performances, just don't go over the top and let it get out of control. Bring it back down with some of the relaxation techniques before it is your turn.

Deal with Anxiety Unrelated to Sport
If you are worried about something other than gymnastics, try to do something to lessen the stress of that situation first. An hour of good quality practice is better than 2 hours of distracted practice. A way to do

this is to make a "Stress List" (*see Appendix page 103 for a copy*). In one column you should list all of your problems and anything stressing you out. It can be something as small as "My room is messy and it's annoying me," to something bigger like "I had a huge fight with my best friend." In the column next to it, you will write one thing you can do to make the situation better. So to continue our example, you could say "When I get home I will clean my room for 5 minutes," and "Text my friend now that I'm sorry and I'd like to talk more later." Knowing that you have a way to deal with your problems may put your mind at ease, at least for right now.

Improve Other Mental Skills
To keep anxiety at a low level, keep your other mental skills at high levels. As an unstoppable gymnast, you will be able to maintain a lower level of stress and also have other skills to fall back on when you do feel stressed. Instead of the anxiety level escalating as the seconds go by, you can use your other mental strengths to bring it back down. Use the confidence building strategies, focus on your goals, see success when visualizing, and stay focused on your cue words (next chapter).

Acceptance
When you go into a competition, be ready to accept the outcome whatever it is. It is nearly impossible to *never* make a mistake or *never* lose. If you hang on to perfection as if the world will end if it doesn't go your way, you will be disappointed most every time. Don't get me wrong though- it is great to strive for perfection! As an unstoppable gymnast, you will achieve it more than most. However, it is not okay to have *zero tolerance* of mistakes. Accept that you made a mistake, and learn from it. Simply determine what your next move is or how to make the situation better. Find the silver lining. At least now you know what not to do, and what to do if it happens again.

Pre-Performance Routine
Doing a consistent routine prior to your performance will help maintain a low level of nerves. Most nerves come from a fear of the unknown (not knowing what's going to happen, the outcome of the event, or what obstacles you will need to deal with), so familiar and well-known actions will give your mind some comfort.

BEFORE: Getting Psyched-Up

The Psych-Up techniques are just the opposites of the relaxation techniques. The most common need for getting psyched up is before practice when there is a lack of adrenaline and/or motivation, or before an early competition when your body is still waking up.

Jump Start

Take just a few quick, shallow breaths (being careful not to hyperventilate or pass out!). Jump up and down, or jog in place for a short time. Take some more quick, shallow breaths. Clap your hands and lightly tap your face. Yell out if the situation allows it. All of this will get your heart rate up, blood flow to your muscles, and air in your lungs.

Motivate Me

Think of what motivates you the most to perform. Go back to the motivation chapter if needed. Why are you here? Why did you get out of bed? What makes you give full effort at practice? What do you want out of yourself and gymnastics today, tomorrow, and in 5 years? Get a vision in your head of whatever the answer is to these questions. Use your visualizing skills and recreate this in your mind with full detail using all your senses. Think of a word to wrap up this image. Yell this word as loud as you can (if the situation allows it- yell into a pillow, in the shower, in your car, or with teammates). Make sure you associate the vision and meaning with the word, don't just yell out an empty phrase.

Motivate Us

The easiest way to get yourself psyched up is to utilize your teammates. Think of a team cheer with your teammates that is meaningful to all of you by using a common team goal as basis for the cheer. Be creative, try to make the cheer more than a simple, "go team!" Come up with a short poem or song for the cheer. Add actions such as arm movements or jumping in unison. Have different people say different lines. The more creative and unique it is to your team, the more psyched-up you'll get.

DURING: Coping Techniques

These are techniques to use during a performance in the middle of the action. These can be used in between events or even while you are performing if needed. Just like visualization, you only need a moment to review a skill or say a cue word.

Relaxation: Deep Breathing
The most well-known form of relaxation is deep breathing. However, it is more than simply breathing deeper. Start by inhaling slowly for 5 seconds. After 5 "gymnastics" seconds (one-gymnastics, two-gymnastics, three-gymnastics...), hold your breath in for 3 seconds. Then begin to exhale slowly for 10 seconds. The numbers aren't as important, but as a general rule exhale more than you inhale. Gradually try to inhale and exhale for a longer length of time. Follow the first part of the relaxation script below for an example of a deep breathing exercise. Do as many breaths as is needed to calm your mind and body.

Relaxation: Progressive Muscle Relaxation (PMR)
PMR is useful for relaxing tight muscles, increasing oxygen and blood flow, and also for falling asleep at night. Adding a stretching routine following PMR could be beneficial as well. To use PMR, first tense all of your muscles one at time starting top to bottom, and then relax all of your muscles one at a time in reverse from bottom to top. The second part of the relaxation script below is an example of PMR.

SCRIPT

This is an example relaxation script that uses deep breathing and PMR. They can be used as one script or separately. Read through the script slowly, pausing after each sentence, to get the full effect.

Focus your attention on your breathing. Notice your chest rise and fall as you breathe in and out. Feel the air fill your lungs and then empty out as you breathe out. Slow down your breathing and make each breath deeper, fuller, more meaningful. Inhale for 5-gymnastics-seconds on your next breath. 1-2-3-4-5... Pause and hold it for 3 seconds before breathing out again. 1-2-3... Then slowly exhale for 10 seconds. 1-2-3-4-5-6-7-8-9-10... After you finish exhaling, forcefully push out the rest of the air in your lungs so that they are completely empty. Again, inhale for 5 seconds on your next breath. Pause and hold it, then slowly exhale for 10 seconds and forcefully push out the rest of the air in your lungs so that they are completely empty. Continue focusing on your breathing, making it slower and deeper. Try to inhale for more than 5 seconds, and exhale for more than 10 seconds. When you inhale, imagine that you are breathing in good, clean, fresh, positive air and holding it allows the positive vibes to go throughout your body. When you exhale, imagine that you are breathing out all the toxins and negativity in your body, and force every little bit out at the end.

Continue breathing slowly and deeply as you change your focus to your muscles. Tense your muscles one at a time starting top to bottom. Keep breathing as you are tensing. Start by tensing your shoulders, tense your chest, your arms, and then clench your fists. Tense your stomach muscles, your butt, your legs, calves, feet, and toes. Now relax your muscles one at a time starting bottom to top. Relax your toes, relax your feet, calves, legs, butt, and stomach muscles. Relax your fingers and hands, your arms, relax your chest, and your shoulders. Continue breathing deeply as you are tensing and relaxing your muscles. Go through again once more- tense your shoulders, chest, arms, fists, stomach, butt, legs, calves, feet and toes. Relax your toes, feet, calves, legs, butt, stomach, fists, arms, chest, and shoulders.

Relaxation Imagery
You can combine visualization and relaxation into one super power. First try imagining calming visions. A calming vision could be:

your happy place

a person you love

soft waves of the ocean

a sunny day in a meadow

the most relaxed you've ever been

Just let your mind wander into any positive, calming places. See your muscles completely relaxed, you are breathing smoothly, and smiling happily. Your other option is to imagine yourself performing everything perfectly. Put your mind at ease by seeing yourself having the performance of your life, as if to say, "Relax. There's nothing to worry about, you've got this down perfectly."

Quick Relaxation
When you really don't have time to do a relaxation technique, you can do a condensed version of the same technique. The quick techniques take

more practice than the regular techniques because you will need to be able to relax faster, but it is better to take a few seconds to be calm and focused than use that time to continue to be stressed out. Take a deep breath while you are waiting or in ready position. 5 seconds in, 3 second hold, and 10 seconds out of a quality deep breath using everything you've got and you'll be more relaxed. If you practice this, you will be able to train your mind and body to fully relax just using the one breath.

Relaxation imagery can be condensed into one vision or one cue word. You won't have time to feel all of the senses one by one in full detail, but you can quickly go through each sense like a checklist. Practice feeling each sense quicker but with the same intensity and clarity.
Example of being relaxed by imagery of the ocean:

Sight... endless blue ocean waves ✓
Sounds... calm crashing water and seagulls ✓
Touch... sand in your toes and sun on your face ✓
Smell... salt water and sunscreen ✓
Taste... cool drink of lemonade ✓

Support from Others
Talk it out with your teammates and coaches. Just venting and hearing the problem out loud can reduce the anxious feelings, make you realize that it isn't as big of a deal as you thought, your teammate or coach will sympathize with you (sometimes that's all you need), or they will provide a different way of looking at it, or a solution you hadn't thought of. All good things!

Focus on Control Cues
When you get stressed out it could be because there is too much going on and you are trying to take control of everything. The more you focus on these outside factors, the more you get stressed out *because they are in fact out of your control.* So to cope with this anxiety, decide what is under your control by doing the following activity:

ACTIVITY

Control Cues:

1. Make a list of everything you could focus on while at practice or a competition. This could be the crowd, the music, loud teammates, opponents, your grips, the beam, the judges, the announcer, your positive thoughts, your negative thoughts, your body, your technique, your scores, your coach, etc. This should be a long list.

2. Now cross off everything out of your control. There shouldn't be too many things left that are truly in your control.

*The items that are left should be: your technique/ your body, and your positive thoughts.

3. When you are stressed out, only focus on these items. You can develop cue words for these and repeat the "control cues" to yourself during a performance when you feel stressed about something out of your power.

The point here is to realize that stressing out by something you cannot control you only make you more stressed. Nothing you do will change that your least favorite judge is on this event, you don't like the song they are playing, or that the beam is a different type than you're used to. Find something you can control, and work towards remedying that situation.

Assessment

Many gymnasts forget about the "after" anxiety, but many look back at what happened and continue to stress about what they did, what they didn't do, the woulda, coulda, and shoulda's of the performance. Even though the competition is over with, the assessment and "after" anxiety of your performance affects your next performance. Use these assessment techniques to stop this vicious cycle.

Attributions

There are 4 things gymnasts can attribute or explain success and failure to: ability, effort, luck and task difficulty. When you succeed, don't blame it on good luck or an easy task- tell yourself it was your ability to succeed and you putting in the effort. Celebrate that! When you fail, don't blame it on your lack of ability- tell yourself it could have been a difficult task, just bad luck, or you may not have put in enough effort (which can change).

Constructive Evaluation

After stressful situations, instead of beating yourself up with "what ifs" and "if onlys", try to revisit the situation and evaluate your performance. Think *constructively* about what you could have done better and make a note to do that next time. You can't change what happened in the past, but you have full control of how you can prepare for your future performances. Don't beat yourself up for doing poorly but also don't just brush it off. Think of the effectiveness of the coping strategies you used. If they didn't work, why not? What could have helped? Either modify the technique to suit your individual needs, or try one of the other techniques.

Pre-Performance

Step 5 is to add a relaxation technique into your pre-performance routine. Remember, your choices could be deep breathing, progressive muscle relaxation, or relaxation imagery.

1. Confidence building technique: _____

2. Motivation purpose: _____

3. Reminder of goals: _____

4. Visualization (summary): _____

_____

5. Relaxation technique: _____

CHAPTER 9
FOCUS

In This Chapter

- Benefits of Precision Focus
- Attention Styles
- Control Cues
- Attention Problems and Solutions
- The Focus Switch
- Choking Under Pressure
- Attention Exercises in Practice
- Pre-Performance Routine

Benefits of Precision Focus

It is pretty common to see a gymnast that is performing well, and then suddenly they fall, miss a skill, or make a mistake. The gymnast proceeds to fall apart. They cannot seem to get back on track and continue to make more and more mistakes. There is a lot going on during practices and meets, and without proper focus you may get trapped in a downward spiral of mistakes.

ACTIVITY

Take a look around you and notice everything that is blue. Memorize the detail, the shade of blue, the location of each blue item in the area. Now close your eyes and visualize everything that is green. You weren't focused on green, so it was as if the objects weren't even there. Same thing holds true for a performance. If you aren't focused on the correct things, you may miss something crucial and make a mistake.

Just as the activity shows, you can be extremely focused on something, but if it's not the right thing it is not helping you at all. Therefore it is important to only focus on the right things.

Attention Styles

Usually when coaches yell, "Focus!" they want you to pay attention to what you are doing because either you are daydreaming or you've made a mistake. If you were daydreaming, it's pretty clear you need to get your mind back on gymnastics and out of the clouds. But if you made a mistake, sometimes it's not clear as to what style of attention you should have used or what you were supposed to focus on and it creates confusion. There are two styles of attention:

Scanning Style
The scanning style is used when you need to pay attention to a wide variety of things. This is your level of focus when you getting ready to take your turn. You are paying attention to your coach, watching other teammates take their turn, listening to corrections and positive feedback that they received, and thinking about what your body needs to do to successfully complete your task. It is important to *scan your surroundings*. You learn more by listening to other teammates' corrections and feedback to know what is correct, what is not, and you'll know visually what incorrect and correct looks like.

Zooming Style

The zooming style will be used when you have 1 or 2 things to focus on. This is your level of focus when it is your turn to perform. Look at the equipment, listen to your coaches' advice, activate your muscles, and think positive thoughts. *Now zoom in with precision focus.* Look at the detail of the equipment and where your hands or feet will be placed. Think of the meaning of your coaches' words of advice; what exactly are they asking of your body and mind? Which specific movements and muscles are needed to execute your skill perfectly? Summarize all of that information in just a couple words. Hold on to your positive thoughts as you begin and <u>zoom in</u> by repeating those couple words, or "cue" words as we will call them.

Control Cues

So let's talk more about what "the right things" are to focus on and what exactly you should be "zooming in" on. When you are performing, there are very few things you should be focused on. We talked about control cues in the last chapter. Let's bring it back for a second look, this time "focusing" on "focus" instead of stress and anxiety.

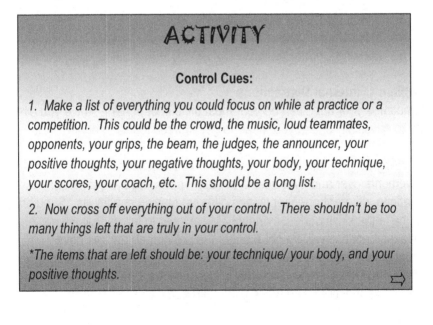

ACTIVITY

Control Cues:

1. Make a list of everything you could focus on while at practice or a competition. This could be the crowd, the music, loud teammates, opponents, your grips, the beam, the judges, the announcer, your positive thoughts, your negative thoughts, your body, your technique, your scores, your coach, etc. This should be a long list.

2. Now cross off everything out of your control. There shouldn't be too many things left that are truly in your control.

*The items that are left should be: your technique/ your body, and your positive thoughts.

> ⇨ *3. When you are losing your focus, remind yourself to focus on YOU. You can develop cue words for these and repeat the "control cues" to yourself during practice or a performance to keep you on task or bring your attention back.*
>
> **When we talked about stress, the point was to realize that stressing out by something you cannot control you only make you more stressed. Now that we are talking about focus, the point is that anything out of your control is simply a distraction. Focus on YOU, YOUR technique/body, and YOUR positive thoughts.**

Attention Problems and Solutions

The 5 main attention problems are:
1. Internal Distractions (*Distracting Thoughts, Negative Thoughts, Past or Future Thoughts, Outcome Thoughts, Don't Thoughts*)
2. Physical Distractions
3. Stress, Pressure, and Physical Fatigue
4. Maintaining Focus
5. Choking Under Pressure

Problem 1: Internal Distractions
Sometimes your mind can be your most difficult opponent. Have you ever had to physically shake your head to get yourself focusing again? Your own thoughts can take you away from gymnastics. Someone once asked me, "Why do gymnasts make mistakes? You practice the same movements over and over again. In other sports you have different situations, different opponents, and different playing conditions. Shouldn't you have the skills perfect by now?" My answer to that is that we make mistakes because we are not robots. We are human and we have thoughts that interfere with our actions. The reason these five internal distractions below are so important is because just one thought can interrupt your actions and make you make a mistake.

a. Distracting Thoughts

These are any thoughts that are unrelated to gymnastics. During practice or during a competition is not the time to be thinking of your boyfriend/girlfriend, a test tomorrow, or what's for dinner. These thoughts are not productive for a performance and prevent you from performing well.

Solutions: Thought stopping and Control cues

b. Negative Thoughts

At your next practice, be aware of every time you have a negative thought. The goal is to recognize specific situations that produce negative thoughts and figure out **why** you become so negative.

Solutions: Thought stopping and Empowering cues. Also review the confidence chapter to reduce the number of negative thoughts throughout the day.

c. Past or Future Thoughts

Thoughts in the past are usually about past mistakes or failures and being worried they will happen again. Thoughts in the future are usually about seeing success or failure before it happens. You may only have your dismount to finish, but if you focus on a vision of you holding a trophy, you may miss the landing as you are daydreaming about the trophy you don't have yet.

Solutions: Thought stopping and Control or Technique cues

> "You have only over the present, right now. Let me prove it to you. I ask you to do this: change the past. Even the smallest, most incidental, least important thing that happened in the past. Go ahead and show that you can change it. The future? Again I ask you, change right now something in the future. Can you? Of course not. Your control exists now, in the present, right here." —John Wooden

d. Outcome Thoughts

When you become overly concerned about the outcome of an event (AA score, finishing 1ˢᵗ place, trophies or medals), you have a *combo* of attention problems:

1. You are paying attention to something out of your control

2. You are paying attention to a non-present thought, specifically the future

Solutions: *Thought stopping and Control or Technique cues*

e. Don't Thoughts

"Don't Thoughts" are thoughts of trying to avoid another thought. "Don't mess up." "Don't fall." "Don't think about pink elephants." You're thinking about pink elephants now right? The mind doesn't register the word "don't." Instead it picks up the most dominant part of the sentence. "Don't mess up" becomes a focus on "mess up," which is exactly what you were trying to avoid.

Solution: *Rephrase the Sentence: If you catch yourself thinking don't thoughts, just switch it to a positive version of the sentence- say what you want to do. Instead of "don't fall," think of actions you should be doing to stay on your feet- stomach tight, reach up, etc. Eventually you'll train your mind to jump over the *don't* part and go directly to thinking of technique.*

Solution: Thought Stopping

Thought stopping can be used for all the internal distractions. You may remember this from the confidence chapter, but we will review. Let's use distracting thoughts as the attention problem.

1. You recognize that your attention is drifting and your thoughts are not helping your performance.

2. The next step is to stop the thought in its tracks. You can think of a big red STOP sign (you can use an actual picture of it if you're struggling with a clear picture), say stop out loud (when it's appropriate), snap your fingers, lightly tap your leg, abruptly shake your head as if shaking the thought out of your mind, or wear a rubberband or hair-tie and snap it when you think negatively.

3. The third step is to replace the "problem" thought with a "productive" thought or a cue.

Solution: Cue Words

"Cues" are one word or short phrases to help keep you focused. We already talked about "Control Cues" which were one word or short phrases for only focusing on what is in your control. Another example would be telling yourself to "relax", which is a "Mood Cue". I've sorted the cue words into 5 categories:

Cue Word	Use if you are feeling...	Purpose of Cue	Examples
Control	Distracted, focused on things you cannot control, excuses, or how this always happens to you	Focus on YOU and what is in your control	"Stay in control", "Focus on ME", "Positive"
Empowering	Negative	Raise your confidence	"Believe", "Power", "Go", "Strong", "Trust"
Mood	Overwhelmed	Calm yourself down	"Relax", "Breathe", "Stay calm", "Beach", your happy place
Motivating	Feeling like shutting down or giving up	Motivate yourself: what makes you most excited at practice	"Getting my kip", "Level 6", "9.0", "States", "Faster, better, stronger", think of goals and personal bests
Technique	Distracted, feeling like you may make more mistakes, or upset about how this will affect your score or awards	An action or instruction to focus only on your body	"Arms up", "Strong legs", "Stay tight", "Fast"

Think of a word for each that *means something to you.* A cue word should eventually evoke an emotional response. Saying "beach" to yourself right now is an empty word; there is no visual image, feeling, or response associated with the word. However, if you imagine how relaxed you are on a tropical beach, the feel of the soft sand between your toes, the calming sounds of the waves, and the happiness that the beach brings you, then after saying "beach" to yourself several times it should evoke calmness in you just by saying the word.

Keep in mind that you should use the correct cue for the situation. In the thought stopping example, the problem was distracting thoughts. For that situation you would use a control cue. Using the "beach" cue would further worsen the problem because the beach does not have anything to do with gymnastics and you are simply continuing to daydream, just about the beach now instead of whatever distracted you initially.

Problem 2: Physical Distractions
Physical distractions are visual and/or verbal distractions such as the crowd, camera flashes, people walking around, or cell phones. These distractions may be more difficult to ignore because they are so obvious and in your face. Internal distractions are like an annoying whisper that bothers and distracts you, while physical distractions could actually be someone yelling in your ear, literally.

Solution: Practice the Distractions
Thought stopping and cues can help with these just like the internal distractions, but since they can be difficult to ignore you will need to take extra precautions. You will need the help of your team or friends for this exercise. During practice, have people on the sidelines that are purposely trying to distract you. They can yell and cheer, talk loudly on their phones, talk as an announcer on the loud speaker, ring a bell (as if overtime on beam), randomly turn the music on loudly, or use any other physical distractions that normally occur. You will start to "desensitize" yourself from distractions; they will just be a part of performing that you are used to. You may need to practice this several times a week, depending on your current focusing abilities.

Problem 3: Stress, Pressure, and Fatigue

When you feel stress, pressure or physical fatigue during a performance, it takes a significant amount of extra effort to maintain attention. When you become physically or mentally tired, your focus turns to how tired you are and away from technique and performing well.

Solution 1: Relaxation then Psych-Up (previous chapter)

Take a moment to use a relaxation technique (deep breathing, progressive muscle relaxation, or relaxation imagery) before the stress or pressure gets out of control or to rest a minute if you are fatigued. Once you get back to neutral, you may need to psych yourself back up, so use the "Jump Start", "Motivate Me", or "Motivate Us" technique to re-energize.

Solution 2: Thought stopping and Technique Cues

Use the technique cue words to keep your mind focused on what your body needs to do, and off of how physically or mentally tired you are.

Problem 4: Maintaining Focus

Just as physical fatigue affects focus, so does mental fatigue. Maintaining focus for an extended length of time, like for a multiple day competition, can be difficult and make you tired of thinking and focusing. It is not feasible to expect to be able to focus for days at a time.

Solution 1: Practice Focus Endurance

Practice focus endurance by imagining yourself during a performance, and each time try to use focus on the performance for a longer period of time. Add 30 seconds at a time and soon your mind will have enough mental endurance to last through a competition.

Solution 2: Make Focus a Switch

Think of focusing as a switch with 3 settings: on, half-off, and off-off. This will help you maintain your focusing skills for when you need them and resting your brain for when you can be relaxing. Keep reading for details.

The Focus Switch

On
When the switch is ON, oh it's ON! It is performance time and there is absolutely no joking around. The switch should definitely be on before and during a performance. The length of time needed before a performance could be a couple minutes to a half hour. You'll need to be ON when you are mentally preparing, physically warming up, and then obviously when competing.

Half-Off
When it is appropriate, turn it "half-off" during breaks. "Half-off" is when you personally are not focused on your skills or technique, but the competition or practice is still going on. This is basically the same as the "scanning style" of attention. You still need to be respectful of others who are performing. You also need to be paying attention to what's going on around you so you know what your coach's instructions are and when you need to start mentally preparing for your next routine. Your coach will definitely not appreciate you goofing off while you are on the sidelines. You can be "half-off" on the team bus, locker room, or during down time such as between events or mid-inning. It is up to you to learn when you need to be focused and mentally preparing and ON, and when it is okay to turn it "half-off".

Off-Off
"Off-off" is when you can completely let go. This is well before the competition or after the last person has finished. It is important to rest your mind before a large or multiple day competition, but again you want time to mentally prepare as well. Find a balance between the three switch settings that allows plenty of both preparation time and mental rest time.

Choking Under Pressure

Think of a time when you were performing and something went wrong. But instead of continuing on, this mistake sent you into an uncontrollable downward spiral. Your performance falls apart and you feel helpless to regain control. More mistakes are made and your performance progressively deteriorates. Sound familiar? To put it bluntly, you choked.

When you choke, it is not a problem with your athletic ability, it is a focusing problem. You were simply focused on the wrong thing at the wrong time (Shelly, 2007).

Solution: Create a Change
Use the Unfocused and Refocusing worksheets in the Appendix on pages 104 and 105 to follow along with Figure H and Figure J.

Unfocused
Learning how to refocus starts with awareness of what happens when you are unfocused. Once you are aware of problem situations, physical and attention changes, and performance consequences, you can do something to **create a change**.

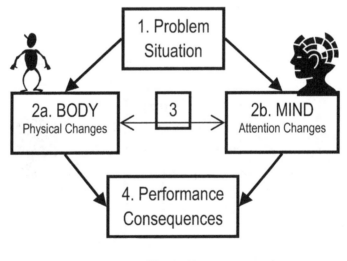

Figure H

1. Problem Situation: Write down a few problem situations that would normally cause you to descend into a downward spiral. Common examples could be a fall on a beam routine at a meet, a certain skill that frustrates you, or if you don't go for a skill you are fearful of.

2. Body and Mind: When you are unfocused, you will experience negative physical and attention changes.
 a. Physical Changes: How does your body react to the problem? Do you get tense, shaky, or sweaty?

 b. Attention Changes: What happens to your attention? Do the internal distractions take over?

3. Body and Mind Interaction: Also be aware that the negative physical changes and negative attention changes feed off each other and help speed up the spiral. When your body starts feeling the stress, your attention may drift to, "Oh no, here come the butterflies," instead of performance-related thoughts. Vice versa, when you think, "This is scary," your body follows suit.

4. Performance Consequences: The negative physical and attention changes, and interactions between the two obviously result in negative performance consequences.

Refocusing
Follow along using Figure J and the Refocusing chart in the Appendix.

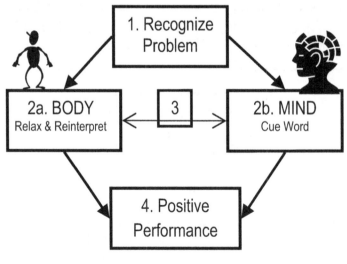

Figure J

1. Recognize Problem: Once you recognize a problem situation that normally causes you to choke or you recognize physical or attention changes, use the following refocusing techniques to prevent or stop a downward spiral.

2a. BODY: Relax and Reinterpret
Relaxation Technique
Create a physical change by using a relaxation technique as described in detail in the previous chapter.

Reinterpret Physical Feelings
Reinterpret your physical feelings using your Optimal Energy Level (OEL). Some energy or nerves are needed to perform well. So if you are feeling the butterflies or are a little shaky, that's ok as long as you feel you are at your OEL. Take your so-called "negative" nerves and reinterpret them as necessary energy.

2b. MIND: Cue Words
If your mind is on overload, create an attention change by focusing on a cue word instead. When your attention drifts it is usually one of the internal distractions, so you'll need to use thought stopping. Then replace the problem thoughts with a cue word that matches how you are feeling. *Review the cue word chart from the Internal Distraction section above.*

3. Body and Mind Interaction: Remember, if you make positive changes in either your attention or physical feelings, the other should improve too. Pick the most pressing problem at the moment, and then if necessary move on to make changes in the other.

4. Positive Performance: If you were successful in creating a change, then you should have a positive performance. This could be a strong finish, a great save on a fall, and/or continuing to stay positive throughout the rest of your routine and the rest of the competition. Continue to relax and reinterpret and focus on cue words for the rest of your whole competition to prevent any further downward spirals.

Attention Exercises in Practice

Just like the "Practice Before Performance Rule" states, you need to practice focusing before you throw these tips into a competition. Since focusing is more difficult under stress, and competitions add stress, it is especially important to integrate the following exercises into your team practice.

Practice with Purpose
Back in my day, we did a lot of drills that I found to be boring or seem like busy-work. I'd ask myself, "Why are we doing this?" However, there is usually a purpose for every drill. If you aren't sure, ask your coach (key: without attitude). Phrase it along the lines of, "Coach, I want to make sure I'm doing this right. What does this drill work on?" Having a purpose will increase your focus and effort.

Take this scenario: You show up to practice and your coach tells your team you will be conditioning for the first hour of practice. Sounds like punishment, right? You all spend most of the time complaining and only giving half your effort because you feel this is totally uncalled for. Had you asked your coach the purpose, he would have told you that when other teams are dragging in the second half of meets and looking tired on their last tumbling pass, he wants his team to be able to push through and finish with strong, flawless routines. Instead, this fires up the team and you all give 100% effort for the full hour, making it a fun competition to see who can do the most pull-ups and leg lifts, and turn into the strongest team in your state.

Practice Competition Settings
Making practice as much like a competition as possible will make competitions no longer as stressful, and allow you to focus like an unstoppable gymnast. Just as I discussed in the physical distractions section, you can have friends and teammates distract you during practice, play a recording of loud crowd noise and announcers, and have people walking around. You can wear your competition uniform, have a shorter preparation time, and even invite friends and family to sit in the bleachers. Do everything you normally would in a competition.

On my gymnastics team in college, we did "stress sets" during practice. Everyone would gather around a piece of equipment and one gymnast would perform their routine. We would cheer loudly and clap as we would in a meet. For some reason it made my heart beat just as loud and fast as it did in a meet. I felt much more prepared when I was able to experience the adrenaline and heart pumping before the actual meet.

If you want to take focusing to the next level of preparation, practice under adverse conditions. Practice with only a few minutes to quickly warm-up, use different music for a floor routine, or use a teammates wrist bands or a spare pair of grips (safely). What if you forgot to bring something to a competition? Try practicing without it so that nothing with shake your focus. Unexpected events cannot stop you.

Pre-Performance

Step 6 is to add a focusing technique into your pre-performance routine. Recite your cue word (control, empowering, mood, motivating, technique) and focus on the meaning.

1. Confidence building technique: _____

2. Motivation purpose: _____

3. Reminder of goals: _____

4. Visualization (summary): _____

   _____

5. Relaxation technique: _____

6. Recite cue word: _____

CHAPTER 10
CONFIDENCE (AGAIN)

In This Chapter

- Benefits of Brilliance
- Composure
- Improved Confidence Building Strategies
- Brilliance Building Strategies
- New Pre-Performance Routine

Benefits of Brilliance

In the first confidence chapter I introduced fifteen confidence building techniques and the idea that everything begins and ends with confidence. The first chapter was about "fake it 'til you make it." This last chapter is about "making it without faking it." I feel that many gymnasts start to build their confidence and then forget to keep going. The biggest part of being unstoppable is having a strong enough confidence to endure multiple mistakes, setbacks, and a lot of frustration. The unstoppable gymnast needs to have a sense of cockiness about them *without arrogance* and therefore a second chapter of confidence is needed to get you to a level I call "brilliance".

Composure

Keeping poised and composed under pressure or in an anger-inducing situation takes incredible confidence. You need to be so secure in yourself to keep your confidence up even after something threatens to take it down. If you allow a mistake, a person, a situation, or anything lessen your confidence, your ability to keep composed is lessened as well.

> *"I have not failed. I just found 10,000 ways that won't work."*
> *-Thomas Alva Edison*

Keeping composed is absolutely critical to becoming an unstoppable gymnast. Many gymnasts will lose their mind after making a big mistake and then every event afterwards is negatively affected because of their lack of focus and confidence. You must learn to let go of mistakes by keeping your cool, your confidence up, and focus intact. Remember that setbacks are temporary. Mistakes will be made, awards will be lost, and you will experience failure. Ordinary gymnasts let these setbacks affect them and take them down. You need to try to understand that setbacks happen, but will pass. This is not a permanent problem. Mistakes don't hold you back, they are just a way of learning what not to do next time.

ACTIVITY

Practice these steps now and use them during practice or even just during daily life for the next time you are frustrated, angry, or make a mistake:

*1. **Stop.** Use all your energy to stop from reacting. Don't say a word and don't make any facial expressions or gestures. Take a step away from the situation. If you are angry with a person, simply tell them you need a minute.*

⇨

⇨

2. Breathe. *Take 3 deep breaths. 5 seconds in, hold for 3, 10 seconds out. Don't rush this, do it full out. If you are competing and don't have time to actually stop, do the breathing as you are performing.*

3. Confidence. *Remind yourself that you are above this. You are a confident and poised gymnast and no setback can lower your confidence. You are unstoppable. Use the best friend test and say something positive to yourself. Remind yourself that showing anger does not help anything and makes you look childish. If you still feel the need to swear or hit someone or yell, then imagine doing this in your head; don't say it under your breath or mouth the words.*

4. Forget it. *Make yourself have short-term memory loss. Forget the mistakes you made, but remember the lessons you learned. Get back to the skill or routine and back to focusing on what is important. You will have bad luck, you'll make stupid mistakes, and the others around you are not perfect. Get over it, move on. Go to plan B, compromise, and make the situation better.*

5. Cue Words. *Use a cue word to get back on track. Review the choking section in chapter 9 if you need help creating a physical or attention change.*

Improved Confidence Building Strategies

By now you should have tried and practiced all the confidence building strategies and you should have found your top 3-5. (If you haven't, go back to chapter 4 and review the confidence building strategies and then return here once you have practiced them thoroughly and found your favorites). Now that you are truly confident, some of the strategies will be too easy now, so you will need to increase the difficulty or move on to the brilliance building strategies.

Embrace a Positive Philosophy

Your motto may not fit your new truly confident self. If it was, "No fear this year," and you don't feel like you are afraid anymore, then it is no longer boosting your confidence, and actually limiting you. Look at the "update your philosophy" strategy in the brilliance building strategies section for ideas for new philosophies.

Positive Encouragement

You've been saying this statement daily (hopefully multiple times). Whereas in the beginning you may have been faking it, now you should believe it. The next level of this is to determine the reasons why your statement is true. Just like the motto, you may need to start saying a different statement that is more appropriate to your new self.

Thought Stopping and Replacement

By now you shouldn't have to stop yourself from saying too many negative statements. Raise the bar- now when you say something even slightly negative or just neutral, change it to something even more positive.

Best Friend Test

Make sure you are still being nice to yourself. Since sometimes best friends can fight like sisters, mean things can still be said. If you need to, when you give yourself criticism, raise the bar- talk to yourself as if you were talking to your grandma or Mother Teresa.

Imagine Perfection

Still imagine yourself performing perfectly, but imagine harder skills too. Remember, this can be an imaginary ideal performance that you wish would happen. So don't hold back, imagine greatness!

Success List

You should have a long list of past successes. Keep adding and updating your list as you achieve more things. Be proud of all your achievements, but stick to imagining only your top successes.

Tracking Progress

You should now have physical evidence that you are improving. Look at the results and be proud of those. Look at how much you have improved since you started, and just think where you'll be if you keep improving at this rate.

State of Mind and Body
You should have some sort of routine down for getting your mind and body ready for a performance. It is easy to slack off on eating healthy or getting enough sleep, so remind yourself that you need to commit to a healthy state of mind and body. You cannot become unstoppable or have a brilliant level of confidence if you are tired, hungover, or malnourished.

Break it Down
Instead of starting at the easiest task, start with a moderate level skill. Work up to the difficult tasks from there. You can still break down difficult tasks into smaller parts, you should just be breaking down tasks that are more difficult than before.

Put it in Perspective
By now, a bad performance shouldn't crush your confidence. It should eventually not affect your confidence at all. You should allow yourself a few mistakes, and then simply change your plan of action. Remind yourself to not get stuck on mistakes and to move toward success.

Attributions
Keep attributing your successes to your ability and effort. You wouldn't have got to where you are without some amount of talent and hard work.

Inspiration
You've been watching teammates and professionals for inspiration, which you can continue to do, but now you may have people watching you to be inspired. Be the good example! Continue working hard on basics and upgrades alike. Younger and lower-level gymnasts are still watching to see if you do a correct split in warm up or if you are goofing off. Still watch uplifting movies and read a good motivational book, because there are always great stories and great people out there to learn from.

Friend and Family Support
Support from family and friends will never stop increasing your confidence and inspiration. Always keep the people who were there when you were struggling because genuine support from true friends is much better than insincere support from fake friends just along for the ride.

Brilliance Building Strategies

This set of strategies is for the gymnast who is confident and ready to take it to the next level. In order to become unstoppable, you will need an extreme level of confidence that does not waver in the face of tough situations. Confidence affects all other mental skills, so a brilliant level of confidence is needed to stay motivated, set difficult goals, visualize absolute perfection, control anxiety, and the ability to stay focused under pressure. Without an unstoppable confidence, you cannot have any other unstoppable skills.

Word of warning: These strategies are for *building brilliance*, not arrogant know-it-alls. Use your confidence for good, not evil. Recognize when you are at a brilliant level of confidence, and when you are just being mean. *Brilliance should never hurt others* and requires a certain amount of modesty before it crosses over into arrogance (Figure K). Pay it forward by helping others around you become more confident as well. It is more important to be a good human being than it is to be good at gymnastics.

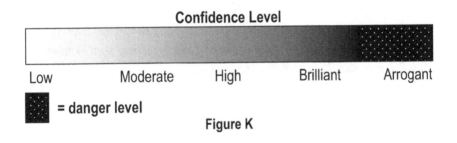

Confidence Level

Low   Moderate   High   Brilliant   Arrogant

= danger level

Figure K

> "*You gain strength, courage, and confidence by every experience in which you really stop to look fear in the face. You must do that which you think you cannot do.*" -Eleanor Roosevelt

1. Achieve the "Impossible"

People around us set standards and limits, and it is up to the great athletes to show that there are no limits to what you can do. For many years people thought running a mile in less than 4 minutes was impossible; that the human body was not capable of it. Then Roger Bannister broke the record in 1954, and many men since then have broken the "impossible" 4 minute mile record (Huber, 2017). People thought a perfect 10.0 was "impossible" until Nadia Comăneci was the first gymnast to be awarded a 10.0 at the 1976 Olympics. She actually earned seven perfect tens at those Olympics! (Armour, 2016). When will people learn that impossible is a word that should never be used in the same sentence as sport?

ACTIVITY

Pick one skill or task you would like to obtain that is very difficult or "impossible" for you to do.

"Impossible" Skill/Task: _____

Decide the steps towards achieving this skill and specifically how you will go about making the impossible possible. You may want to make this your long-term goal (from chapter 6).

1. _____

2. _____

3. _____

4. _____

When you achieve this skill, your confidence will certainly go from blah to brilliant. If you do not achieve this skill (PS. Give yourself plenty of time to achieve it), well, you came pretty darn close, and a lot further than you thought you ever could, right? "Impossible" is not that far out of your reach now.

2. Show Confidence on the Outside

Now that you have become confident in yourself on the inside, your behavior, expressions, and actions should match on the outside. You may have formed habits when you lacked confidence, and now you need to change these habits.

Look at your posture when you stand. Do you slouch, turn your toes in, or look downward? Or do you stand tall and proud with your chin up? Posture is the easiest way to tell how someone is feeling. Make sure your confidence shines through via your body language.

Communicate confidently. Have eye contact when you talk to others, and avoid nervous fidgeting. Blushing is rather involuntary, but remind yourself that what you have to say is important and you deserve to have your voice heard. Avoid crossing your arms as that is a sign that you are closed off to what the other person has to say, and you may unintentionally put them on the defense. Talk slowly and clearly so that your message comes across as solid and secure, and also to keep your voice from cracking.

Realize that others cannot see how you are feeling on the inside. Many times I have been extremely nervous for a public speaking event, but when talking to people in the audience after they had no idea I was nervous. Be grateful that butterflies are invisible and keep your mind on your message.

3. Break Through the Brick Wall

You may find that reach a limit to your confidence, as if a brick wall was in your way preventing you from reaching the brilliant level. In order to become unstoppable, you need to break through this brick wall. Your own brick wall could be anywhere on the spectrum in Figure L. Lucy's brick wall could be between low and moderate, and Susan's brick wall could be between high and brilliant. Use the activity on the next page and find it within yourself to make it to that next level of confidence.

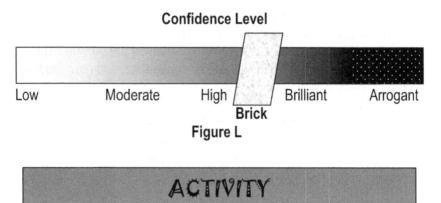

Confidence Level

Low   Moderate   High   Brilliant   Arrogant

Brick

Figure L

ACTIVITY

Everyone's brick wall is made up of different barriers, obstacles, or "bricks." A brick is anything that is holding you back from greatness and allowing yourself to attain brilliant confidence. Determine what these are by asking yourself these questions:

1. When you fail at something or make a mistake, what do you tell yourself? Is this productive or holding you back? _____

_____

2. Look at your 8 words that describe your self-concept (Chapter 4), specifically the negative ones. Which qualities are holding you back? Why aren't you the "perfect you"? What qualities or abilities do you wish you could have? _____

_____

3. Do your emotions hold you back? (Ex: Sadness, anger, jealousy, regret) _____

_____

4. Do you care what others think of you? Why?

_____

_____ ⇨

⇨

Use the questions to help fill in each brick on the brick wall below with something or someone that is holding you back from making it to the other side (Brilliant Confidence Level). Don't necessarily just put each answer in a brick, but use your answers to help pinpoint what exactly your bricks are. (Examples: Negative self-talk, jealousy, self-conscious of my hair, have to work harder than everyone else, lack of flexibility)

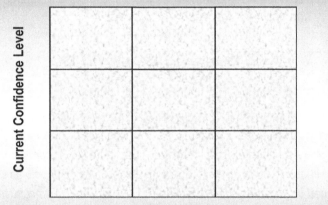

Figure M

Now that you are aware of what is holding you back, you can do something about it. For each brick, decide what needs to be done to throw the brick away; establish what actions or changes will better the situation. Use positive thinking and thought stopping, a new philosophy, cue words, and the rest of the brilliance building strategies to help you throw away all of your bricks. Cross the bricks out as you are able to throw them away.

4. You Control Your Confidence

Start each day knowing that you are in charge of your confidence. Others cannot take it away through negative comments, behaviors, or opinions. Only you have the power to build it up or tear it down- and you better be building it up!

> *"No one can make you feel inferior without your consent.*
> *Never give it."*
> *-Eleanor Roosevelt*

Side Note: Don't confuse negative comments and criticism (see #5). Negative comments are meant to hurt you, criticism is meant to help. Some criticism is laced with negativity, so just separate the message from the negativity and only take the message to heart.

ACTIVITY

Everyone is born with a survival instinct, a natural tendency to do anything to survive when threatened. In the animal world, the weakest of the group becomes lunch for the lions. The same thing happens in social situations- no one wants to be the weakest. When people feel threatened by you, their survival instinct will kick in. They say negative comments in an attempt to hurt you, bring you down, and make you weaker, so that they aren't the weakest of the group. If you believe these people or let them get to you, they win- you become defeated, weak, lack confidence, and lunch for the lions.

Think of your confidence as a star. The more confidence you have, the brighter it is. The less you have, it becomes damaged or it gets dimmer. The intention of someone's negative comment is to take away some of your confidence, and to damage your star, so that your star becomes dimmer than theirs (and easier for the lions to catch you).

As an unstoppable gymnast, you have a bright star (1). This can be threatening to other gymnasts and they may say negative comments in an attempt to try to make your star dimmer and feed you to the lions (2).

Figure N (1&2)

⇨

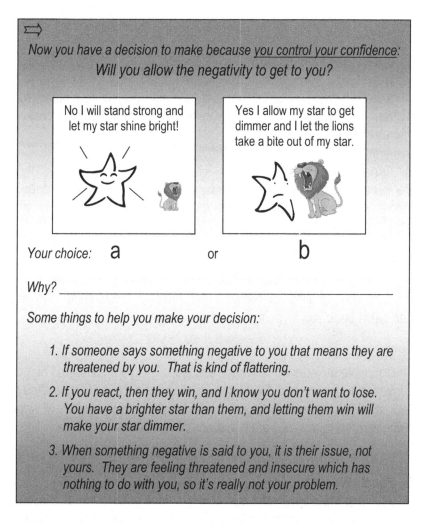

Now you have a decision to make because <u>you control your confidence</u>: Will you allow the negativity to get to you?

No I will stand strong and let my star shine bright!

Yes I allow my star to get dimmer and I let the lions take a bite out of my star.

Your choice: **a**   or   **b**

Why? _____

Some things to help you make your decision:

1. If someone says something negative to you that means they are threatened by you. That is kind of flattering.

2. If you react, then they win, and I know you don't want to lose. You have a brighter star than them, and letting them win will make your star dimmer.

3. When something negative is said to you, it is their issue, not yours. They are feeling threatened and insecure which has nothing to do with you, so it's really not your problem.

5. Cool Down the Criticism

Like most people you have a little person in your head who constantly points out your shortcomings. Some criticism is okay. Some will keep you on your toes and will push you to be better. But too much will just make you feel defeated and like you can't ever can anything right. Make sure any criticism you give yourself is <u>constructive</u>. If the criticism is just an observation of something you did wrong, that's not helping you; it should help you improve upon something. You can also cool down the criticism by bragging to yourself. Follow each negative criticism with a bragging statement. If you say to yourself, "That was terrible technique!" follow it with, "But the move before that was pretty fantastic."

6. Update Your Philosophy
Most likely your new confident self doesn't match your motto anymore. Choose something a little cockier that will make you set your standards higher. Use Figure K to help you stay on the good side and not cross over into arrogant.

A. Assume Success
Begin each practice or competition by assuming that you will succeed. As long as you've trained hard and are mentally preparing adequately, you have no reason to believe you won't succeed.

B. Better, Stronger, Faster
Have the idea in mind that you are awesome, and that every day you practice, you get a little bit better, a little stronger, a little faster. No one can catch up to you if you train hard every day!

C. No Excuses
Unstoppable athletes do not make excuses. Set your standards higher. Strive for perfection and don't let yourself make excuses for mistakes or lack of effort. Excuses such as "I had a lot going on today," or "I'll work twice as hard tomorrow," are not acceptable at the brilliant level.

7. Secret Weapon
You have something special, something unique about yourself that other gymnasts do not have; a mental or physical edge that others do not have. It may be a certain skill or task you perform well, talent during pressure situations, your endurance, strength, or your agility, or how fast you are able to improve or learn new skills. Whatever it is don't be afraid to exploit it, be proud of this ability. Giving it a name such as secret weapon will put help emphasis it and keep the focus on your strengths.

ACTIVITY

Think of your strengths, and then choose the one you feel is your strongest strength for your secret weapon.

What are your strengths?

_____   _____

_____   _____

_____   _____

_____   _____

What is your strongest strength, your "secret weapon"?

_____

When it is time for you to use your secret weapon, unleash it! You know you are good at this, so go for it, it's your time to shine!

8. Train like a Champion

Training as hard as you can during every practice will ensure that your confidence is brilliant during a competition. In your mind you know you have done everything you could have possibly done to prepare for the meet. There are no doubts in your mind of, "Well, if I had only practiced this more…" No. You are prepared. Also, don't rely on talent alone. If you are a naturally talented gymnast, good for you. But you still need to work harder than everyone else. You've been given a gift. Not working hard to improve upon that gift is a huge waste. You can do so much more with your talent with hard work.

> *"It's not that I'm that talented, it's that I have this ridiculous work ethic. Meaning that I absolutely positively refuse to accept anything less than 100% of what I can achieve."*
> *-Will Smith*

New Pre-Performance Routine

The final step is to add a brilliance building technique to your pre-performance routine so that the last thing you think of is how great you are, and how great you are going to perform.

1. Confidence building technique: _____

2. Motivation purpose: _____

3. Reminder of goals: _____

4. Visualization (summary): _____

   _____

5. Relaxation technique: _____

6. Recite cue word: _____

7. Brilliance building technique: _____

In chapter 3 you described your current pre-performance routine. I have suggested 7 techniques to use for your new pre-performance routine. You can simply use these 7 techniques, or you can modify them to fit in with actions, thoughts, or rituals you were using before that you found to be beneficial or comforting.

Write your new pre-performance routine here:

_____

_____

_____

_____

_____

_____

_____

The New Unstoppable You

Be more aware of your thoughts and actions.

Make a commitment to your sport.

TRAIN HARD.

Trust yourself.

See success.

Think positive.

Set goals.

Relax.

Breathe.

Always try again.

Believe in yourself.

Be UNSTOPPABLE.

<u>Appendix</u>

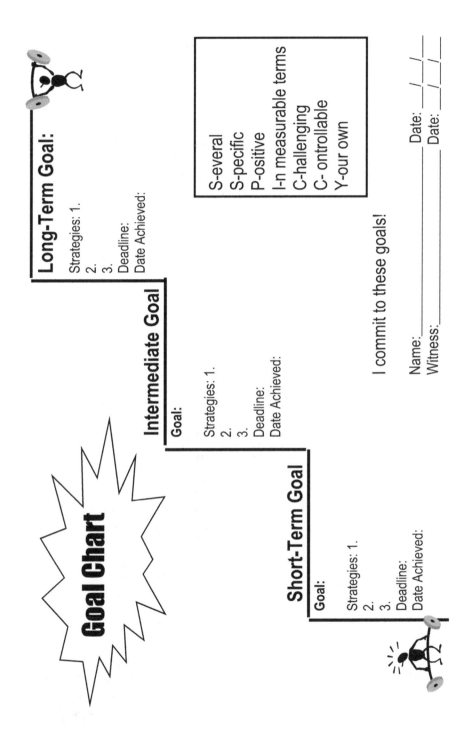

Goal Chart

Long-Term Goal:

Strategies: 1.
2.
3.
Deadline:
Date Achieved:

S-everal
S-pecific
P-ositive
I-n measurable terms
C-hallenging
C- ontrollable
Y-our own

Intermediate Goal

Goal:

Strategies: 1.
2.
3.
Deadline:
Date Achieved:

Short-Term Goal

Goal:

Strategies: 1.
2.
3.
Deadline:
Date Achieved:

I commit to these goals!

Name: _____ Date: ___/___/___
Witness: _____ Date: ___/___/___

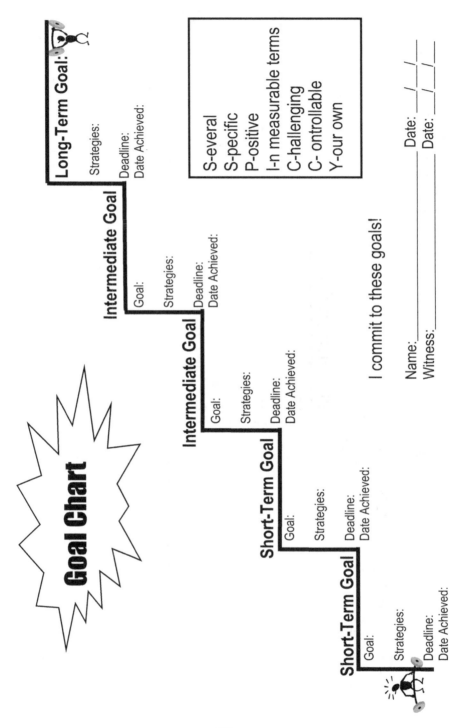

Goal Chart

Long-Term Goal:
Strategies:
Deadline:
Date Achieved:

S-everal
S-pecific
P-ositive
I-n measurable terms
C-hallenging
C- ontrollable
Y-our own

Intermediate Goal
Goal:
Strategies:
Deadline:
Date Achieved:

Intermediate Goal
Goal:
Strategies:
Deadline:
Date Achieved:

Short-Term Goal
Goal:
Strategies:
Deadline:
Date Achieved:

Short-Term Goal
Goal:
Strategies:
Deadline:
Date Achieved:

I commit to these goals!

Name: _____   Date: ___/___/___
Witness: _____   Date: ___/___/___

Stress List

	What's Stressing You	What are you going to do about it?	When?	✓
1				
2				
3				
4				
5				
6				
7				
8				
9				
10				

Use Chapter 8: Anxiety Management, page 61-62

Unfocused

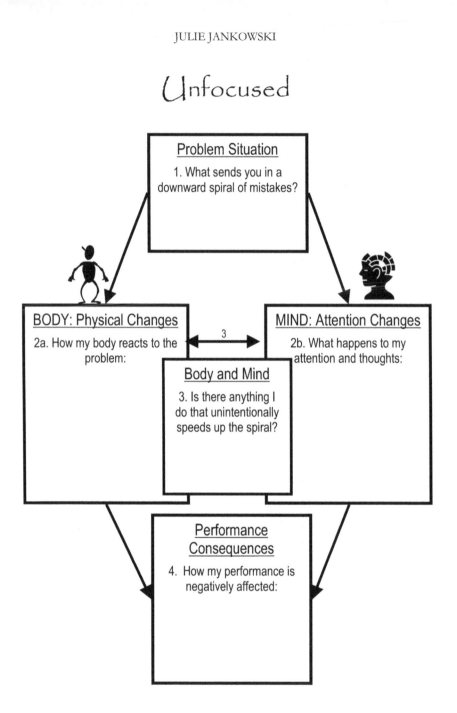

Problem Situation

1. What sends you in a downward spiral of mistakes?

BODY: Physical Changes

2a. How my body reacts to the problem:

3

Body and Mind

3. Is there anything I do that unintentionally speeds up the spiral?

MIND: Attention Changes

2b. What happens to my attention and thoughts:

Performance Consequences

4. How my performance is negatively affected:

Use Chapter 9: Focus, page 78-81

Refocusing

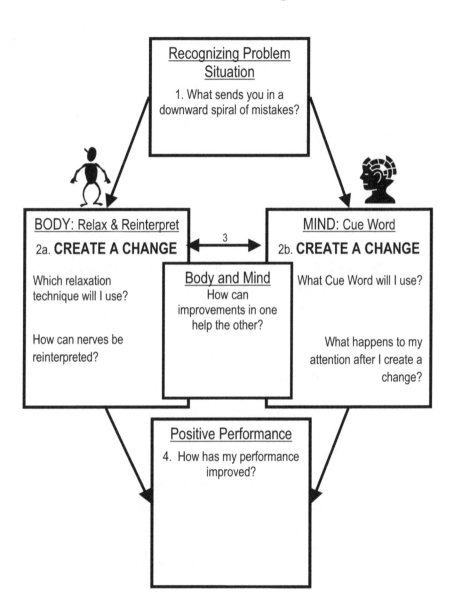

Use Chapter 9: Focus, page 78-81

References

Anderson, D.C., C.R. Crowell, M. Doman, and G. Howard. "A systematic analysis of feedback, goal-setting, and work-contingent praise as applied to a university hockey team." *Journal of Applied Psychology*. 73. (1988): 87-95.

Armour, Nancy. "40 years after perfect 10, gymnast Nadia Comaneci remains an Olympic icon." *USA Today*, Gannett Co., Inc, July 20, 2016, https://www.usatoday.com/story/sports/olympics/rio-2016/2016/07/20/10-gymnast-nadia-comaneci-olympics-montreal/87357146/.

Borg, Gunnar. *Borg's Perceived Exertion and Pain Scales*. Champaign, IL: Human Kinetics, 1998.

Brobst, Brandilea and Philip Ward. "Effects of public posting, goal setting, and oral feedback on the skills of female soccer players." *Journal of Applied Behavior Analysis*. 35. (2002): 247- 257.

Burton, Damon. *Evaluation of Goal Setting Training on Selected Cognitions and Performance of Collegiate Swimmers. Thesis (Ph.D.)* University of Illinois at Urbana-Champaign, 1983.

Burton, Damon. "Winning isn't everything: Examining the impact of performance goals on collegiate swimmers' cognitions and performance." *The Sport Psychologist*. 3. 2 (1989): 105-132.

Creasy Jr., John Wayne. *An Analysis of the Components of Mental Toughness in Sport. Dissertation*. Virginia Polytechnic Institute & State University, 2005.

Dorfman, H.A. and K. Kuehl. The Mental Game of Baseball. New York: Diamond Communications, 2002.

Duda, Joan L. "Relationship Between Task and Ego Orientation and the Perceived Purpose of Sport Among High School Athletes." *Journal Of Sport & Exercise Psychology*. 11. (1989): 318-335.

Elferink, G., C. Visscher, K. Lemmink, and T. Mulder. "Relation between multidimensional performance characteristics and level of performance in talented youth field hockey players." *Journal of Sports Sciences (London).* 22. 11/12 (2004): 1053-1063.

Filby, William C.D., Ian W. Maynard, and Jan K. Graydon. "The effect of multiple-goal strategies on performance outcomes in training and competition." *Journal of Applied Sport Psychology.* 11. 2 (1999): 230-246.

S. Fourie, S. and J.R. Potgieter. "The nature of mental toughness in sport." *South African Journal for Research in Sport, Physical Education and Recreation.* 23. 2 (2001): 63-72.

Gentner, Noah. "Goal Setting Obstacles." Ithaca College, 2007, Ithaca, NY.

Gould, D., R. Eklund, and S. Jackson. "1988 U.S. Olympic wrestling excellence: I. mental preparation, precompetitive cognition, and affect." *The Sport Psychologist.* 6. 4 (1992): 358-382.

Gould, D., D. Guinan, C. Greenleaf, and Y. Chung. "A survey of U.S. Olympic coaches: variables perceived to have influenced athlete performances and coach effectiveness." *The Sport Psychologist.* 16. 3 (2002): 229-250.

Gould, D., L. Petlichkoff, K. Hodge, and J. Simons. "Evaluating the effectiveness of a psychological skills educational workshop." *The Sport Psychologist.* 4. 3 (Sept 1990): 249-260.

Gould, D. and E. Udry. "Psychological skills for enhancing performance: arousal regulation strategies." *Medicine & Science in Sports & Exercise.* 26. 4 (Apr 1994): 478-485.

Gould, Daniel, et al. "Factors affecting Olympic performance: Perceptions of athletes and coaches from more and less successful teams." *The Sport Psychologist.* 13. (1999): 371-394.

Gould, D., V. Tammen, S. Murphy, and J. May. "An examination of U.S. Olympic sport psychology consultants and the services they provide." *The Sport Psychologist*. 3. (1989): 300-312.

Harrell, Kirsten, Psy.D. "The Power of Guided Imagery." *Think Positive! Blog*, ipopin.com, 12/4/2006, http://ipopin.typepad.com/think_positive/2006/12/i_read_a_great_.html.

Huber, Martin Fritz. "A Brief History of the Sub-4-Minute Mile." *Outside Online*, Mariah Media Network LLC, June 9, 2017, https://www.outsideonline.com/2191776/brief-history-sub-4-minute-mile.

Jones, Graham, Sheldon Hanton, and Declan Connaughton. "What is this thing called mental toughness? An investigation of elite sport performers." *Journal of Applied Sport Performers*. 14. (2002): 205-218.

Jones, G. and A.B.J. Swain. "Predispositions to experience debilitative and facilitative anxiety in elite and non-elite performers." *The Sport Psychologist*. 9. (1995): 201-211.

Lambert, Sarah M., Dennis W. Moore, and Robyn S. Dixon. "Gymnasts in training: The differential effects of self-and coach-set goals as a function of locus of control." *Journal of Applied Sport Performers. 11. 1 (1999): 72-82*.

Locke, E. A., K.N. Shaw, L.M. Saari, and G.P. Latham. "Goal setting and task performance: 1969–1980." *Psychological Bulletin, 90.* 1 (1981): 125-152.

Mahoney, Michael J. and Marshall Avener. "Psychology of the elite athlete: An exploratory study." *Cognitive Therapy and Research*. 1. 2 (1977): 135-141.

Meyers, M., A. Bourgeois, A. LeUnes, and N. Murray. "Mood and psychological skills of elite and sub-elite equestrian athletes." *Journal of Sport Behavior*. 22. 3 (1999): 399-409.

Meyers, M., LeUnes, A., & Bourgeois, A. "Psychological skills assessment and athletic performance in collegiate rodeo athletes." *Journal of Sport Behavior.* 19. 2 (1996): 132-146.

Orlick, T. and J. Partington. "Mental links to excellence." *The Sport Psychologist.* 2. 2 (June 1988): 105-130.

Reilly, T., A. Williams, A. Nevill, and A. Franks. "A multidisciplinary approach to talent identification in soccer." *Journal of Sports Sciences (London).* 18. 9 (2000): 695-702.

Scarnati, J. T. "Beyond technical competence: Developing mental toughness." *Career Development International.* 5. 3 (2000): 171-176.

Siebold, Steve. *177 Mental Toughness Secrets of the World Class: The Thought Processes, Habits and Philosophies of the Great Ones.* Hong Kong: London House, 2005.

Shelley, Greg. "Visualization Principles." Ithaca College, 2007, Ithaca, NY.

Shelley, Greg. "Choking Under Pressure." Ithaca College, 2007, Ithaca, NY.

Swain, A., and G. Jones. "Effects of goal-setting interventions on selected basketball skills: A single-subject design." *Research Quarterly for Exercise and Sport.* 66. (1995): 51-63.

Thomas, Patrick R. and Gerard J. Fogarty. "Psychological skills training in golf: The role of individual differences in cognitive preferences." *The Sport Psychologist.* 11. (1997): 86-106.

Ungerleider, S. and J. Golding. "Mental practice among Olympic athletes." *Perceptual & Motor Skills.* 72. 3 (1991): 1007-1017.

Wanlin, C.M., D.W. Hyrcaito, G.L. Martin, and M. Mahon. "The effects of a goal setting package on the performance of speed skaters." *Journal of Applied Sport Psychology.* 9. (1997): 212-228.

Wang, L., S. Huddleston, and L. Peng. "Psychological skill use by Chinese swimmers." *International Sports Journal*. 7. 1 (2003): 48-55.

Ward, Phillip and Michael Carnes. "Effects of posting self-set goals on collegiate football players' skill execution during practice and games." *Journal of Applied Behavior Analysis*. 35. 1 (2002): 1-12.

Weinberg, R. S. and D. Gould. *Foundations of Sport and Exercise* Psychology (3rd ed.). Champaign, IL: Human Kinetics Publishers, Inc., 2003.

Weinberg, Robert, Thomas Stitcher, and Peggy Richardson. "Effects of a Seasonal Goal-Setting Program on Lacrosse Performance." *The Sport Psychologist*. 8. 2 (1994): 166-175.

Williams, A. and T. Reilly. "Editorial: Searching for the stars." *Journal of Sports Sciences*. 18. 9 (2000): 655-656.

Williams, Jean M. *Applied sport psychology: Personal growth to peak performance*. Boston, MA: McGraw-Hill, 2005.

Yukelson, David, PhD. "What is mental toughness and how to develop it?" 2008, http://www.mascsa.psu.edu/dave/Mental-Toughness.pdf.

ABOUT THE AUTHOR

Julie Jankowski started her own gymnastics career at a Mommy and Me class, competed in the USAG gymnastics program through level 7, was on her high school's very first gymnastics team, and continued competing at the college level before eventually retiring after an injury.

Julie's experience as a gymnast profoundly affected her life. She decided her career goal would be to become involved in sport psychology in order to help other gymnasts become more mentally tough than she felt she was able to in her gymnastics career. She chose sport psychology as her major in college and graduated with a Master's degree in Exercise Science with a concentration in Sport Psychology.

Julie was a Sport Psychology Consultant for several years, then tried out a few different career paths before she finally returned to gymnastics as a coach. She resides in Buffalo, NY with her husband Jon and sons Easton and Brody. Writing this book will be a fulfillment of a dream she has always had! Julie feels she has finally found her calling as a gymnastics coach and is now living the dream!

Made in the USA
Middletown, DE
07 December 2019